IN SEARCH OF ANCIENT GODS

My Pictorial Evidence for the Impossible

Also by ERICH VON DÄNIKEN:

Chariots of the Gods?
Gods from Outer Space
Gold of the Gods

In Search
Of Ancient Gods

MY PICTORIAL EVIDENCE

FOR THE IMPOSSIBLE

Erich von Däniken

Translated by Michael Heron

G. P. PUTNAM'S SONS   NEW YORK

FIRST AMERICAN EDITION 1974

Copyright © 1973 by Econ Verlag

Translation Copyright © 1973 by Michael Heron
and Souvenir Press. All rights reserved

Published simultaneously in Canada
by Longman Canada Limited, Toronto

Second Impression

SBN: 399-11346-0

Library of Congress Catalog Card Number: 73-93725

PRINTED IN THE UNITED STATES OF AMERICA

Men have been fascinated by space since time immemorial. What did those pinpoints of light in the heavens mean? Surely those glittering strings of beads seemed to form outlines of animals? Or were they human beings? Could the lights be the homes of the gods?

Our galaxy consists of about 100,000 million fixed stars, but it is only a tiny part of the Milky Way, which contains some twenty galaxies within a radius of one-and-a-half million light years. (One light year is roughly equal to six *million million* miles.) Even this figure is small in comparison with the approximately 1,500 million galaxies that have been recorded so far. Where does it come from, this incredible mass of matter that is scattered throughout the universe over many millions of light years? Even today the answers to that question are no more than theories.

There is the Big Bang theory. All matter was compressed into one primordial atom, which created such pressure on its own core that it exploded. The galaxies originated from the shower of pieces produced by this heavy mass of matter. In 1842 Christian Doppler proved that if a source of light moves away from the observer, the spectrum shows a shift towards red. The 'Doppler effect' makes it possible to measure the speed of the stars. In 1929 Edwin Powell Hubble was able to show that the universe is expanding. He proved that the speed at which a galaxy recedes increases the further away it gets. Thus astronomers were able to deduce that all matter originally existed in a condensation of hydrogen of extremely high density at one point. Then came the Big Bang. Ever since then all the pieces of matter have been hurtling away from each other.

Carl Friedrich von Weizsäcker was the author of the widely accepted theory that all the suns and planets were 'born' from a cloud of gas that consisted of 99% hydrogen and helium, and 1% heavy elements. The galaxies built themselves around the heavy elements in a system of whirlwinds.

The Steady State theory (1948) assumes that the universe is stationary and that new matter originates from the void, so to speak, but so slowly that its genesis cannot be recorded.

According to the 'Oscillation' theory, matter contracts and expands like a heart beating. Its rhythm lasts 60 milliard years. What *is* the answer?

1

Red and yellow gods, black and white gods, gods with almond-shaped eyes and slits for ears, with fat bellies and round heads, with black blood, with dragon's faces. Gods with terrifying ray-guns, gods in celestial chariots that shine (like chromium), spindle-thin figures with antennae, gods with wheels attached to their thighs, gods floating above water and clouds, crouching in spheres like embryos, riding on flying snakes, striding through Hades, lording it among the stars, gods ascending in pillars of cloud, travelling in vimaanas (Sanskrit for flying machines) and 'disappearing into the sky in pearls'. Jealous, envious, malicious, outraged, martial gods.

What does it all mean? Are these images of the gods inspired by hallucinations common to peoples all over the world? Are they products of the need all peoples feel for a religion or are they really attempts to reproduce realities which have been seen, but misunderstood?

Carl Gustav Jung (1875–1961) interprets the mythical observations of ancient peoples as the development of an archetypal consciousness. According to him the 'collective unconscious' is the expression of both good and evil, pleasure and punishment, love and death. However psychology does not help me very much in the field I have chosen. It can pursue its research into the psyche – hence its name – successfully, beca•se its methods are applicable there; but these methods are not applicable when reality demands an accurate interpretation. In my view, myths are the oldest traditional accounts of human history, in other words accounts of what was once reality.

These traditional accounts brought forth strange fruit. For example, there is the Babylonian Etana epic, which mainly comes from the clay tablet library of the Assyrian King Assurbanipal (669–626 BC). The actual origin of the epic is unknown, but parts of it are included in the much older Epic of Gilgamesh, written in the Akkadian language. The Sumerians began to write down their past in 2300 BC. Just as Enkidu, the hero of the Epic of Gilgamesh, was carried up above the earth by a god, Etana also floats high in the air. Here are the essential passages describing this from the Etana epic:

The eagle said to him, to Etana:

'My friend, I will carry thee to the heaven Anus,

Lay thy breast on my breast,

Lay thy hands on the pinions of my wings,
Lay thy sides on my sides.'

. . . . . .

When he had carried him aloft for a while,
The eagle spoke to him, to Etana:
'Look, my friend, how the land has changed,
Look at the sea at the side of the world mountain.'
'The land there looks like a mountain, the sea
has become like a watercourse.'

. . . . . .

When he had carried him aloft a little longer,
The eagle said to him, to Etana:
'Look, my friend, how the land has changed.'
'The earth looks like a plantation of trees.'

The eagle (god) climbs higher and higher with Etana, and keeps
on asking him to look down and say what he sees. Finally he
can only see 'as much as a hut' of the land and the vast sea
becomes as tiny as 'a courtyard'. The last stage of what is
probably the oldest eye-witness account from space is fascinating:

'My friend, look down and see how the world has changed.'
'The land has turned into a cake
And the vast sea has become the size of a breadbasket.'
And yet again he carried him higher and said:
'Look down and see how the land has *disappeared*.'
'I look down and see how the earth has *disappeared*
Nor do my eyes feast on the vast sea.
My friend, I do not want to ascend into heaven,
Stop, that I may return to earth.'

Does this eye-witness account of a flight, a description of the
earth receding, *have* to be interpreted 'psychologically'?
I am firmly convinced that 'gods' in mythology can only be a
synonym for space travellers, for lack of a more accurate name
for the flying phenomena. Time and again the texts begin:
'Take up thy pen and write,' or: 'Watch carefully what I show
thee, and tell it to thy brothers and sisters.'

Men in the remote past did not know what to make of these accounts; they were intended for later generations. The addressees were ourselves! With our knowledge of space travel and our familiarity with photographs taken from satellites, we can recognise the facts in these stories. We know what our earth looks like from a great height. To us, the image of 'porridge and water-trough', with which the earth seen from a great distance is described in the Epic of Gilgamesh, is simply what the first astronauts saw. Truths and realities have found their way into sagas, legends, myths and holy scriptures. We must try to extract the kernel from the shell of tradition. In the end we shall have the true prehistory of the human race in our hands. Everyone ought to be interested in this knowledge. The questions 'Where do we come from' and 'Where are we going' concern all the peoples on this earth.

The universe has been 'traversed' for millennia in mythology. The names of the constellations of Ursa Minor and Ursa Major, Cygnus, Hercules, Acquila, Hydra and the names of the twelve signs of the zodiac date to the third millennium BC.

Zeus (in Latin, Jupiter), the supreme lord of heaven, is called lightning-hurler and loud thunderer in Homer (eighth century BC). The Nordic god Thor is also a thunderer. In the Indian sagas Rama and Bhima travel up the cloud-mountains 'riding on a monstrous ray', amid tremendous noise. In the Aztec legend, Mixcouatl, the 'thundering cloud snake', comes to earth on the fourth day of creation and begets children. Even today the Canadian Indians tell of a thunder-bird that visited their ancestors in the dim past and that this thunderbird came straight from the skies. Tana, too, the god of the New Zealand Maori legends, is a thunder god who decides his battles in space with 'lightning'.

The usual explanation is that our primitive ancestors created their gods as representations of natural events, such as clouds and lightning, thunder and earthquakes, volcanic eruptions and sun and stars. If we look at the rock drawings of our early ancestors, this explanation seems to be carried *ad absurdum*.

These are not natural events stylised into gods, these are portrayals of gods-cum-men! If god or gods were 'believed' to be natural phenomena (and depicted as such), then our naïve ancestor cannot have accepted the idea that he was God's image. We have no reason to believe that those ancestors of ours who thousands of years ago wrote down either what they had experienced or what they had been told were weak in the head. It is a fact, and no one will dispute it, that mankind's oldest myths and legends tell us about gods flying in the sky. It is a fact that all the stories of creation assert, with variations, that man was created by gods from the cosmos, after they had come down to earth from heaven. The creation was not a home-made affair.

In Greek mythology, Zeus has to fight the dragon Typhon before he can found a new world order. The god of war, Ares (in Latin, Mars), the son of Zeus, was always in the company of Phobos and Deimos, symbols of fear and dread. Today Mars's two moons are called Phobos and Deimos. Even the delightful Aphrodite (in Latin, Venus), daughter of Zeus, cannot bestow her favours on the king's son Adonis, until the war in the universe has ended. In the South Sea legend of the Tawhaki islanders, the lovely maiden Hapai comes down to earth from the seventh heaven to spend her nights with a 'handsome man'. This chosen lover has no idea of the maiden's heavenly origin until she gets pregnant by him. Not until the happy event has occurred does she reveal that she holds the rank of goddess and comes from the stars.

No, when the god-men have reached earth after battles in outer space, they behave far too 'naturally' for them to have been incarnations of natural events.

2   This 'Unknown male figure' in fired clay is 5½ inches high. It dates from the Obed period, the fourth millennium BC and is on show in Baghdad Museum. The insect-like eyes, which are in complete contrast to the realistic proportions of the body, are a remarkable feature. What model could the prehistoric artist have had when he depicted this mythological figure? And waistcoats that looked like uniforms were not common in 4000 BC.

3

4

3 A winged cherub (ivory). Similar ivory carvings, often decorated with gold and precious stones, were found in hundreds in the region of Sumeria and dated from at least 800 BC.

4 This four-winged figure, commissioned by Cyrus the Great (*c*. 600 BC), stands near Persepolis. Here the ability to fly is attributed to the ruler, although no-one in his period is supposed to have seen a being flying.

5 A cylinder seal from the first millennium BC. If flying men were not supposed to exist then, flying horses are preposterous!

6 A winged Assyrian sphinx (eighth century BC).

7 Pieces of jewellery like this gold pendant were placed in the sarcophagi of Egyptian mummies. The helmeted head of an aviator, with two wings behind it, perpetuates mankind's eternal dream of being able to fly.

8 These two winged creatures (with lions' feet!) were found near Arslan Tasch in Syria.

5

6

7

15

8

9 This female being, insect-headed, but otherwise human, dates to the fourth millennium BC (Iraq Museum, Baghdad). The same strange combination of man and animal constantly reappears in mythology and prehistoric art.

10 Did the Babylonian women of the second millennium BC parade the beaches of the Persian Gulf in present-day fashions?

11

12

11–12 The same motifs are found on both the dragon monolith at Villahermosa (Mexico) and on the Assyrian relief of a 'winged spirit'. Both beings can fly, the former sitting in the dragon, the latter with his own wings; both are holding something that looks like a basket. Was there communication between the artists over a distance of 8,000 miles?

13 This silver figure, $2^2/_5$ inches high, from Mesopotamia (2000 BC) is known to archaeologists as the 'Sacrifice Maker'. To whom was he sacrificing? Does his star-studded robe give us a clue?

14 This 10-foot high stele is supposed to portray the Assyrian King Assurbanipal (British Museum, London). Curiously enough all the Assyrian kings have the same standard face and mysterious symbols always float between sun and moon.

13   14

15

15 When a winged being needs a name, archaeologists simply call it a 'spirit'. Like all his comrades, this one wears a piece of jewellery on his wrist that looks very like a watch. It would be very easy to make a collection of watches from Assyrian spirits!

Whole volumes could easily be filled with representations of flying, fire-breathing gods who landed on the earth and impregnated women, for these mythical deities rapidly appeared in engravings and paintings. There is no end to the pictures of winged beings holding strange appliances in their hands. Pictures of unknown solar systems and their planets appear on Sumerian, Assyrian and Babylonian cylinder seals. (Cylinder seals made of hard or semi-precious stones were used by the peoples of the ancient east to seal their property.) It does not surprise me that these representations correspond to the 'coded' descriptions in the ancient texts, because they have their origin in *a* reality. Here is the story of a landing by a spaceship. The Spanish chronicler Pedro Simon included it in his collection of the myths of the Chibchas (men) from the east Colombian cordilleras:

> It was night. There was still something
> Of the world. The light was enclosed in a big
> 'Something-house' and came out of it.
> This 'Something-house' is 'Chiminigagua'
> And it concealed the light inside it so that it came out . . .

One of the cuneiform texts, addressed to the Egyptian sun god Ra, says:

> Thou couplest under stars and moon. Thou drawest
> The ship of Aton in heaven and on earth like the tirelessly
> revolving stars and the stars at the North Pole that do not
> set.

An inscription on a pyramid reads:

> Thou art he who directs the sun ship of millions of years.

This quotation comes from the Egyptian *Book of the Dead*, an ancient collection of texts that contains instructions for life after death:

I am the great god who begets himself.
The secret might of my name
Creates the heavenly order of the gods.
The gods do not impede my progress.
I am yesterday.
I know tomorrow.
The fierce battle the gods fight with one another
Takes place according to my will.

One of the oldest prayers in the *Book of the Dead* reads:

O world-egg, hear me!
I am Horus of millions of years!
I am lord and master of the throne.
Freed from evil, I traverse the ages
And spaces that are endless.

'The Songs of Creation' in the *Rigveda*, the oldest Indian book, contain this passage:

In those days there was neither being nor non-being . . .
The life-powerful that was enclosed by the void,
The ONE, was born by the power of a hot urgency.
Who knows for sure, who can proclaim here,
Where it originated, from whence this creation came?

17

17 Victory stele of the Assyrian King Asarhaddon (681–669 BC). Above him are various mythological gods, a winged sun, an octagonal star and between them flying beings.

Sumerian myths tell of gods who travelled in heaven in barks and fireships, came down to earth, impregnated the Sumerians' first ancestors and then returned to the stars. Sumerian tradition has it that the gods brought writing and the formula for making metal. Utu, the sun god, Inanna, the goddess of love, and Enlil, the god of the air, came from the cosmos. Enlil violated the earth maiden Meslamtaea and impregnated her brutally with divine seed. Not all the gods went down in legend as perfect gentlemen!

18

19

20

18 Terracotta relief of a Babylonian woman from the first millennium in a snappy pair of pants!

19 Winged deity from the first millennium BC (Tell Halaf).

20 Alabaster relief of a king flanked by winged beings (ninth century BC).

21

22

21   Bird with human head and helmet. There are two seated figures in its wings (British Museum).

22   Winged beings flank the 'Tree of Life'. Surely the geneticist should recognise a schematic representation here? Four bases (adenine, guanine, cytosine and thymine) produce sugar and phosphoric acid molecules, and these in turn amino acids. It is quite obvious that this is no normal 'tree'.

Sumerian history can only be dated to the nearest several centuries. The Sumerians are supposed to have come to Mesopotamia from Central Asia about 3300 BC. In those days, when Europe was still slumbering in the Neolithic, the Sumerians developed writing. Perhaps they needed sealed documents and accounts for the management of the temple. Pottery developed with the advent of the potter's wheel; weapons came on to the market with the technique of boring holes in stone. About 3000 BC the intelligent Sumerians invented the art of making cylinder seals. Cylinder seals were stamps from one to six centimetres long, which were usually worn on a chain round the neck by their owners, because of their great value. The Sumerians rolled these seals on clay vessels, stamped documents with them or used them to receipt taxes due to the temples, which also acted as Treasuries. Cylinder seals were always of a high artistic standard, and the earliest seals found to date bear mythological figures and symbols: birdmen, fabulous animals and spheres in the sky. Scholars say that these representations are abstractions. Yet I wonder whether the Sumerians really *began* their art with abstractions, for abstraction is normally considered to be an advanced stage in art. The god Shamash is depicted with burning torches on his back. He holds a strange object in his hand. In front of him twinkles a star from which a straight line goes down (to earth?). Shamash has one foot on a cloud, the other on a mountain; he is flanked by two remarkable columns on which small animals are keeping watch. A cylinder seal christened 'The Temptation' is preserved in the British Museum. Two clothed figures sit opposite each other, one with antenna-like horns growing out of its head. Between them grows a stylised tree with branches. A snake is twined at the foot of the tree. Why 'Temptation'? Were the godparents thinking of the temptation in paradise? What an absurd association of ideas! This cylinder seal is much older than the biblical Genesis. I am rash enough to see in it a different kind of 'Fall'. A god (astronaut) is handing on knowledge to a pupil; perhaps he is explaining how he is always to be reached through his high frequency antennae? Several cylinder seals from Sumerian and Babylonian times are illustrated in the following pages. They invite the reader to reflect and compare.

23

24

25

23–25 Cylinder seals. Are these really supposed to be abstractions? Winged beings, stars and spheres.

26

27

26–31 Cylinder seals, the first miniature memorials of mankind, are impressive evidence of memories of divine visits from the universe. Acceptable interpretations going beyond the 'mythological figure' syndrome have not yet been put forward, but it is impossible to miss the space attributes such as planetary systems, winged spheres, figures floating in space and apparatuses smacking of technology.

28

29

30

31

Behold the people is one . . . and this they begin to do: and now nothing will be restrained from them, which they have imagined to do. *Genesis xi, 6.*

Until the first hydrogen bomb was exploded by the USA in November 1952, near the Marshall Islands, its inventors had worked behind barbed-wire fences under conditions of the utmost secrecy. It is much the same now with geneticists and biologists working on hereditary factors in their laboratories, for the genetic code is the hydrogen bomb of the future. An artificially-produced virus, released into the atmosphere by an anarchistic revolutionary movement, could mean the end of the world. When the moon astronauts returned to earth in 1969, they spent three weeks in quarantine. Scientists were afraid that they might introduce extraterrestrial viruses against which the human organism would have no defences. But – synthetic viruses are already being produced today!

In 1965 Professor Sol Spiegelmann of the University of Illinois isolated the virus phi-beta, a result which nature cannot achieve, because the natural virus always reproduces itself. And in 1967 scientists at Stanford University, Palo Alto, California, succeeded in synthetising the biologically active nucleus of a virus. Following the genetic pattern of the virus phi X 174, they constructed from nucleotides one of the giant DNA (deoxyribonucleic acid) molecules that control all vital processes. The scientists at Palo Alto introduced synthetic virus nuclei into host cells. The artificial viruses developed there like natural ones; they bullied the host cells into producing millions of new viruses. In the meantime Professor Arthur Kornberg succeeded in deciphering thousands of combinations of the genetic code for the virus phi X 174. Had 'life' been 'produced' in the Californian laboratories? But a virus is not a 'living organism' according to the classical definition, because it has no metabolism, it does not develop. A virus does not eat, nor does it multiply by fission. As a parasite, it multiplies in foreign cells by reproduction. We could breathe a sigh of relief – man cannot create life after all! We were wrong! In May 1970, Har Gobind Khorana of the University of Wisconsin told the Federation of American

Societies for Experimental Biology that he had succeeded in making a *gene*, the bearer of hereditary information. His colleague Salvador E. Luria said: 'In principle at least, made-to-measure man has become possible much sooner than we thought he would.' Will it ever be possible to make man to measure?

Since the middle of the nineteenth century we have known that the cell is the bearer of all vital functions. Cells multiply a million-fold by cell division; they are all building components of the organism. If anyone wants to change the organism, he must begin with the smallest building unit, the cell. Starting

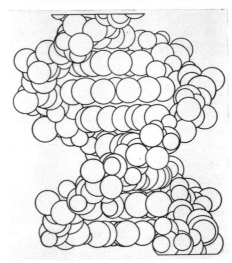

32

from here all the great biological discoveries of modern times were made. The miraculous world of the cell was first revealed by the electron microscope. It was discovered that each organism has a specific number of chromosomes, which have their own specific shape. The genes in the chromosomes are programmed with hereditary factors. But how is a gene constructed?

In 1962 James D. Watson, Francis H. C. Crick and Maurice H. F. Wilkins received the Nobel Prize for the answer to that question. These three men demonstrated that the molecules inside each gene assume the shape of a double helix. The DNA double helix consists of sugar and phosphoric acid molecules. The sugar molecule is made up of four bases: adenine, guanine, cytosine and thymine. Watson and his collaborators realised that the sequence of the four bases in the DNA is fixed, for sugar and phosphoric acid molecules develop from the bases in a definite sequence. The variable sequence determines the arrangement of the twenty-to-thirty amino acids in a protein molecule. The logical conclusion was obvious: to alter the construction of an organism, one would have to alter the sequence of the four bases in the DNA. Clearly such manipulation is incredibly difficult. A DNA macromolecule (a gene-hereditary factor) consists of several thousand nucleotides. (A nucleotide is formed from one of the four bases, together with sugar and phosphoric acid molecules.) There are about 1,000 million pairs of nucleotide bases distributed among forty-six chromosomes in a single human cell. With such endless possible variations it seems almost impossible to decipher the (hereditary) information programmed in a gene and then alter it. Nevertheless, I am convinced that the molecular geneticists, who are working today as enthusiastically as the inventors of the hydrogen bomb, will succeed in finding the genetic code for changing simple forms of life within the next few years. Professor Marshall W. Nirenberg of the National Institute of Health, who played a decisive part in the discovery of the genetic code, says he is sure that it will be possible to programme cells with synthetic genetic information within the next twenty years. Once the first step of altering simple forms of life has been taken, the second, namely the genetic mutation of highly complicated organisms and man, will soon follow. After all, we live in the computer age and computers can supply the molecular geneticists with the millions and millions of calculations required in a flash.

What has this brief excursion into molecular genetics to do with *my world*? A very great deal. I want to establish a connection that my readers will understand. One day it will be possible to change hereditary factors (including our own!). Basic research has already shown that. Surely an extra-terrestrial intelligence that had mastered the technique of space travel and was thousands of years ahead of us in matters of research could easily have been far more advanced than we are in molecular genetics? I also wish to oppose the arrogant assumption that (terrestrial) man is the lord of creation. But if alien cosmonauts possessed knowledge that we are just beginning to acquire, they could have endowed our first ancestors with intelligence by manipulating the genetic code. Admittedly, it is still only a speculation of mine that hominids became intelligent by an artificial mutation using the genetic code. The new men thus manipulated would indeed have become intelligent *suddenly*, as in the abracadabra of the Creation stories; they would have been endowed at once with consciousness, memory and a flair for handicrafts and technology. Seen in that way the Sumerian cylinder seals depicting the tree of life assume a new aspect. Are they not embarrassingly like the double helix?

33

34

35

36

37

33–43 An interesting book could easily be compiled simply of illustrations of cylinder seals. In these few pages I can only give the reader an impression of the almost compulsive similarity of the motifs. Let us hope some Professor of Biochemistry will suggest cylinder seals to one of his students as a subject for his thesis!

38

39

40

41

42

43

44

44 Gods in a 'flying machine' above the tree of life and a half-moon. There is no acceptable explanation of the rocket-like apparatus and the floating spheres on the left-hand edge of the picture.

45 Winged mythological gods; above them a flying machine with spheres. Where did the creators of these miniature memorials get their subjects from? (British Museum.)

What would actually happen on a planet where technology was non-existent if a spaceship landed there? How would farmers and soldiers react to the terrifying sight? How would priests, scribes and kings – or whoever formed the élite on the planet – react?

Something terrible has happened. The heavens have opened. Strange beings in a gleaming house have descended on a glistening ray accompanied by frightening noises. They must be gods. Scared out of their wits, the 'natives' watch the new arrivals in their clumsy spacesuits from a safe hiding-place. The only light they know is the light of their own campfires, the light from primitive lamps and torches. Here before their blinded eyes night becomes brighter than day. The strangers have power over divine suns (the cosmonauts set up a group of searchlights). The strangers make the earth burst open, as further proof that they really have divine powers (that is, they make a normal test explosion to see what mineral wealth there is). Then the un-invited guests dart lightning around them (they flash a laser beam). Now the watchers cannot believe their eyes; with a roaring clatter a veritable skyship that can float over land and sea rises into the air and disappears into the clouds (that is, a helicopter takes off). They hear a tremendous voice echoing far over the land like the voice of god (the commanding officer gives his orders over a loudspeaker). Those are all impressions that spacemen might make on the inhabitants of a planet untouched by technology. Naturally the 'natives' recount what they saw. Naturally scribes write it down, not without embellishing the facts with religious flourishes. Thousands of years pass. Learned men find and interpret their writings. They do not understand the phenomena described: divine suns, lightning rooting up the earth, skyships? Their ancestors must have suffered from hallucinations, they must have had mental attacks or seen visions. Because what ought not to be cannot be, the accounts must be fitted into a neatly arranged system, and the most reckless flights of fancy are indulged in to make the troublesome 'phenomena' plausible enough for everybody to be able to 'believe' them. Religions, cults and ideograms are all pressed into service, indeed they are invented *ad hoc* if existing ones do not provide a suitable catalogue number for the inexplicable events. When the ancient texts finally fit the conventional pattern, people must 'believe' in the interpretation. Doubt is heresy. All I can say about this method is: 'Thinking strictly forbidden!'

If we can believe the Old Testament scholars, a terrifying event took place in the year 592 BC and the prophet Ezekiel described it. (It has become a showpiece in my chain of evidence!) Let Ezekiel speak:

> Now it came to pass in the thirtieth year, in the fourth month, in the fifth day of the month, as I was among the captives by the river of Chebar, that the heavens were opened . . . And I looked, and, behold, a whirlwind came out of the north, a great cloud, and a fire infolding itself, and a brightness was about it, and out of the midst thereof as the colour of amber, out of the midst of the fire. Also out of the midst thereof came the likeness of four living creatures. And this was their appearance; they had the likeness of a man. And every one had four faces, and every one had four wings. And their feet were straight feet; and the sole of their feet was like the sole of a calf's foot: and they sparkled like the colour of burnished brass . . . Now as I beheld the living creatures, behold one wheel upon the earth by the living creatures . . . The appearance of the wheels and their work was like unto the colour of a beryl: and they four had one likeness: and their appearance and their work was as it were a wheel in the middle of a wheel. When they went, they went upon their four sides: and they turned not as they went. As for their rings, they were so high that they were dreadful: and their rings were full of eyes round about them four. And when the living creatures went, the wheels went by them: and when the living creatures were lifted up from the earth, the wheels were lifted up . . . And when they went, I heard the noise of their wings, like the noise of great waters, as the voice of the Almighty, the voice of speech, as the noise of an host . . . and above the firmament that was over their heads was the likeness of a throne, as the appearance of a sapphire stone: and upon the likeness of the throne was the likeness as the appearance of a man above upon it.

Five years ago I gave a technical and therefore, in my opinion, realistic explanation of this text from Ezekiel. What Ezekiel saw and described was a spaceship and its crew. Everybody laughed at me. I refused to let my confidence be shaken and supported my explosive theory in *Return to the Stars* with further quotations from the book of the prophet. My critics shifted from ridicule to savage attacks. Many journalists, who obviously did not know where their pens were leading them, joined in the attacks by the religious clique. The Swiss Professor Othmar Keel, of the University of Freiburg, claimed in his book *Back from the Stars* that my technical explanations were completely without foundation and turned up his arrogant nose – in the true style of the old school. Incidentally, the corps of Old Testament scholars are by no means united in their exegeses of the smoke-fire-lightning-thunder-and-throne phenomena in the books of the Old Testament, except on one point, a technical explanation is *out*. Professor Keel understands the 'phenomena' as ideograms, while Professor Lindborg takes the same events to be hallucinatory experiences. Dr A. Guillaume sees natural events in the epiphanies of God, yet his colleague Dr W. Beyerlein would like to interpret them as parts of the ritual at Israelite religious festivals. Dr Fritz Dummermuth at least sneaked into the periodical of the theological faculty of Basle that 'on closer examination the accounts in question cannot be easily reconciled with natural phenomena of a meteorological or volcanic kind,' and observed that 'the time has come to approach things from a new point of view if biblical research is to make any progress in explaining them'.

Now I can take a provocatory step further and claim that traditional biblical scholarship will soon have no part to play in the interpretation of Ezekiel. The Old Testament, like a lot of other 'holy scriptures', talks about many incidents which really belong to the sphere of technical research. Whenever 'God' or 'gods' actually show themselves in actual surroundings, they always do so to the accompaniment of fire, smoke, earth tremors, light and noise. For my part, I cannot imagine the great omnipresent god needing a vehicle to get from one place to another. God is inconceivable, eternal, almighty and omniscient.

God is spirit. And God is good. Then why should he terrify the objects of his love with demonstrations of power such as are described in the Old Testament? Above all, as God is omniscient, he knew perfectly well that the phenomena handed down in the texts would be interpreted by the children of the twentieth century – in the light of their own knowledge. Almighty God is timeless. He knows no yesterday, no today and no tomorrow. I find it blasphemous to insinuate that the true God must await the result of an operation initiated by himself or that he could expose it to misinterpretation. *Such a God* must know how the traditional texts will be explained in later times – by ourselves, for example. If people wish to regard God as sacrosanct, they cannot call him as a witness for the crown for all the interpretations that have been made until now.

All right then. The prophet Ezekiel saw and described a spaceship. As commanding officer and crew spoke the prophet's language – otherwise he would not have understood them – it is logical to assume that the crew had observed the inhabitants of the region over a long period, learning their language and studying their customs. Contact was only made with Ezekiel after careful preparation. According to the account in the Old Testament, the experiences and the reports of them took place over twenty years. Ezekiel was an observant chronicler. He was impressed by the gleam of the metal and the noise of the ship, by the extended stilt-like legs of the landing capsule, by the glowing condensers of the nuclear reactor. The commanding officer's shining protective suit looked like 'burnished brass'; he compared the rotor blades of the helicopter to 'living creatures'. He found it astonishing that the wheels of the vehicle 'went upon their four sides: and they turned not as they went'. He tries several times to find words for the noise that accompanies the 'phenomenon', but as he cannot conceive of louder noises, he uses similes such as the noise of great waters or the noise of a host. If Ezekiel had suffered from hallucinations, as some scholars say, he would not have had to struggle for words and images to express the inconceivability of the noise. As far as I know, hallucinations are not accompanied by noises, nor do they affect the environment. This fact alone should have made the exegetes of the old school think twice, as should this accurate description of a technical process:

. . . when the living creatures went, the wheels went by them: and when the living creatures were lifted up from the earth, the wheels were lifted up . . . When those went, these went; and when those stood, these stood; and when those were lifted up from the earth, the wheels were lifted up over against them.

A 'miracle'? Of course not! When a helicopter takes off, it's hard for its wheels to remain on the ground!

I have already said that my interpretation of Ezekiel's text has become a showpiece in my chain of evidence. Josef F. Blumrich, an engineer in charge of the NASA construction research group at Huntsville, Alabama, owner of several patents to do with rocket construction and holder of the NASA Exceptional Service Medal, uses his engineering knowledge to prove the existence of Ezekiel's spaceship in his book *And the Heavens Opened* and confirms it by his familiarity with the latest technological developments. In the Introduction to his book, which fascinates by its accurate and sober textual analysis, Blumrich says that he really wanted to refute the claims I made in *Chariots of the Gods?*, but after lengthy study of the text he had to admit defeat, although the effort turned out to be richly rewarded, fascinating and enjoyable.

The quintessence of Blumrich's investigations was as follows:

The conclusions reached show us a spaceship that is not only technically possible, but also very sensibly adapted for its mission. We are surprised to find a stage of technology that is in no way fantastic, but rather falls almost within the field of our presentday potentialities, in other words one that is only a little way ahead of our time. In addition the conclusions show a spaceship that was used in connection with a command module in orbit round the earth. The only fantastic thing is that such a spaceship was tangible reality more than 2,500 years ago!

The key to the explanation of Ezekiel's account lay, as Blumrich writes, in a detailed analysis of the parts of a spaceship described by him and their functions, using the knowledge available in the present stage of rocket and spaceship technology. I do not wish to reproach the Old Testament scholars for not knowing how to calculate or (re-)construct, but I do oppose them for continually selling us the same old theological claptrap as the *ultima ratio* of ostensible scholarship. Blumrich's demand that engineers should be called in when constructions or similar objects have to be judged is absolutely right. Scholarship concerns itself with questions near the limits of possibility, but matters within these limits come within the province of the engineer, especially the constructor, because he has to develop the actual making of even the most advanced constructions from the very beginning. 'Consequently he is also the man who can best deduce the purpose and use of a construction from its outward appearance.'

Engineer Blumrich also writes:

It is possible to infer the general appearance of the spaceship described by Ezekiel from his account. Then an engineer can set aside his report and reconstruct a flying machine with the same characteristics. If he then shows that the result is not only technically possible, but also practical and well thought-out in every respect, and moreover finds details and processes described in Ezekiel's account that tally perfectly with his own conclusions, one can no longer speak simply of indications. I discovered that Ezekiel's spaceship has very credible dimensions.

And these are the dimensions of the spaceship described by Ezekiel:

Specific impulse	I_{sp} =	2,080 sec
Weight of construction	W_0 =	63,300 kg
Fuel for return journey	W_9 =	36,700 kg
Diameter of rotor	D_r =	18 m
Total power developed by rotor	N =	70,000 HP
Diameter of spaceship proper	D =	18 m

46

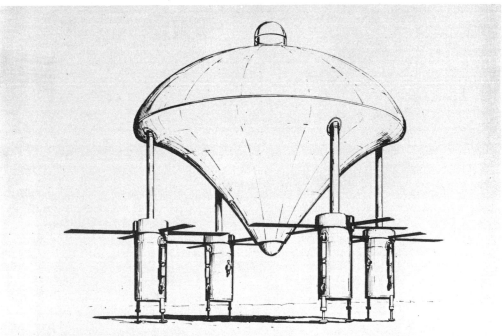

47

46–47 These two illustrations are only apparently contradictory. The one from an old bible gives a fanciful but non-technical impression of the Ezekiel 'phenomena', whereas the one by the NASA engineer Josef F. Blumrich reproduces what Ezekiel described in a technical way.

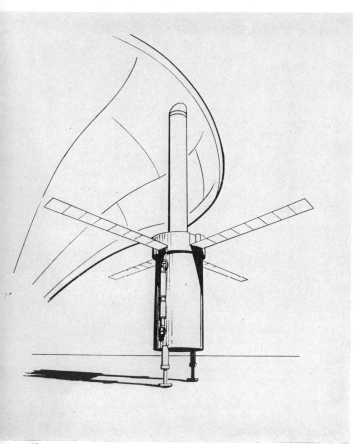

49

48

48–49 '. . . And their feet were straight . . . and they sparkled like the colour of burnished brass' says the prophet Ezekiel. In the technical reconstruction hydraulic sprung legs emerge from the straight legs with flat supporting discs which ensure an adequate distribution of weight. We have all seen similar landing feet in action on moon vehicles.

50–53 '. . . their appearance . . . was as it were a wheel in the middle of a wheel.' When Mr Blumrich, the NASA engineer, followed the data given in Ezekiel, he hit on a sound technical solution. The wheel was divided into different segments, with each segment ending in a small axis. As each axis could be turned to right or left, this construction could even manoeuvre at right angles. As only one segment touches the ground at a time, the Commanding Officer could set the wheels in motion not only forwards and backwards, but sideways as well.

50

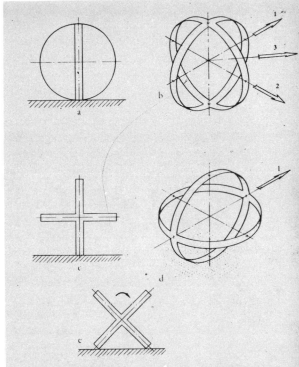

51

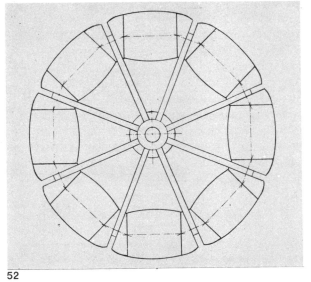

52

53

The work of the censors appointed in Rome about 440 BC was valiantly taken over by the religious communities of the early Christian church. The editors of the Bible acted as their own censors. They did not allow *all* existing manuscripts to be included in the book of books. Learned theologians know that the Apocrypha (Greek: hidden scriptures), made up of Jewish and Christian supplementary writings, were excluded from the canon, as were also the pseudepigrapha, Jewish scriptures from the century before and after Christ, that ought to belong to the Old Testament but were not accepted either in the Bible or in the canon of apocryphal scriptures of the Catholic church. Presumably they were not 'holy' enough for the biblical censors to give them a place in *our* Old Testament.

One of the sections of the Bible withheld from us is the Book of Enoch (Hebrew: the initiate). One of the original fathers, according to Moses, a pre-Flood patriarch, the son of Jared, he has been overshadowed for thousands of years by his son Methusalem (Hebrew: man of the missile), who is supposed to have been 969 years old. After his service on earth, the prophet Enoch rose into heaven in a fiery chariot. It is a good thing that he left his records behind, for they give us deep insights into the earliest mysteries of astronomy, tell us about the origin of the gods and supply details of the 'Fall'. The Book of Enoch is supposed to have been written in Hebrew or Aramaic originally, but the manuscript has not been found so far. If things had gone the way the Fathers of the Church wanted, no one would ever have heard of the Book of Enoch. But by a freak of fate the Early Abyssinian Church had accepted Enoch's scripture in their canon! The news reached England in the first half of the seventeenth century, but not until 1773 did the African explorer J. Bruce bring a copy back to England. Subsequently some dubious copies in Latin came into circulation. The book was translated into German for the first time at Frankfurt in 1885. In the meantime fragments of a very early Greek transcript were discovered. Comparison of the Ethiopian and Greek texts showed that they tallied, so we can assume that we now possess an 'authentic' Enoch.

I own a translation of Enoch published in Thübingen in 1900. To the best of my knowledge there is no more recent translation. That is a pity, for the Thübingen version is complicated and difficult to understand. The turn-of-the-century translators were so baffled – one can sense this – when confronted with the astronomical series of figures and the genetic manipulations described that they accompanied ten lines of Enoch by at least twice as many lines of notes and gave several possible translations.

Enoch, chapters 1–5, announces a Last Judgment. It claims that the divine God will leave his heavenly abode to appear on earth with his angelic host. Chapters 6–16 describe the fall of the rebel angels; they give the names of the angels (spacetravellers) who couple with the daughters of men against the orders of their God (captain of the spaceship). In chapters 17–36 Enoch's travels in different worlds and distant firmaments are described. Chapters 37–71 contain all kinds of parables which the gods told the prophet. Enoch was enjoined to hand them down to later generations, for the men of his time were unable to understand the technical connotations, which were aimed at a later age. Chapters 72–82 give astonishingly accurate details of the orbits of sun and moon, intercalary days, the stars and the functioning of the heavens. The remaining chapters contain conversations between Enoch and his son Methusalem, whom he warns of the imminent Flood. Enoch ascends into heaven in a fiery chariot to give the book a 'happy ending'.

I hope the following literal extracts will publicise the Book of Enoch, which the Fathers of the Church withheld from us, and in my role of *enfant terrible* I should like my 'audacious' commentaries on them to give new stimulus to thought.

> Chapter 14: They bore me up into the heavens. I entered and walked until I came to a wall built of crystal stones and surrounded by tongues of fire; and it began to strike terror into me. I went into the tongues of fire and came to a large house built of crystal stones. The walls of that house were like unto a floor paved with crystal stones, and its floor was of crystal. Its roof was like the paths of the stars and lightning, with fiery cherubs in between. A sea of fire was round its walls, and its doors burned with fire.

I think there is little doubt that in this case a ferry ship took Enoch from earth to the command module which was in orbit round the earth. The gleaming metal hull of the spaceship seemed to him to 'be built of crystal stones'. Through a heat-rejecting fortified glass roof he could see the stars and meteorites, and also observe the flashes from the steering jets of smaller spaceships. ('Its roof was like the paths of the stars and lightning, with fiery cherubs in between!') Enoch also saw the dazzlingly bright spaceship wall on the side facing the sun. Or was he astounded by the blinding jet exhausts of braking rockets? Undoubtedly he was afraid of having to step into the fire. He is all the more surprised a moment later to find that the interior of the 'house' is as 'cold as snow'. Obviously, our reporter Enoch knew nothing of the possibilities of pressure compensation or air-conditioning, techniques which the strangers used and were familiar with.

> Chapter 15: And I heard the voice of the most High: Fear thou not, Enoch, thou righteous man and scribe of righteousness ... go thou and speak to the guardians of heaven who have sent thee in order to intercede for them. For they should really intercede for men, and not men for them!

There is no doubt that Enoch is standing in front of the Commanding Officer, to whom the 'guardians' have brought him. Who are these 'guardians'? Ezekiel mentions these strange figures, they appear in the Epic of Gilgamesh, they haunt the fragmentary texts of the mysterious Lamech Scrolls which were found in caves high above the Dead Sea. In the last-named, Lamech's wife, Bat Enosh, swears to her husband that she conceived in a natural way and that she had had nothing to do with a 'guardian of heaven'. Now the same guardians figure in Enoch's book! The Commanding Officer makes two remarks worthy of reflection. First he addresses Enoch as 'scribe', that is he counts him as one of the small élite capable of writing; second, the Commanding Officer says with unconcealed scorn that the 'guardians' should intercede for men, not men for the 'guardians'. The Commanding Officer goes on to explain what he means:

> (Say to the guardians) . . . why have ye left the lofty holy

heavens, slept with women, defiled yourselves with the daughters of men, taken wives unto yourselves and done like the children of earth and begat sons like giants? Although ye were immortal, ye have defiled yourselves with the blood of women, and begat children with the blood of the flesh, lusted after the blood of men and produced flesh and blood, as they do who are mortal and perishable.

In other words, the space travellers were much older than the inhabitants of earth and apparently immortal. Long before the encounter with Enoch, the Commanding Officer had obviously left a crew of his 'guardians' on the blue planet earth and then gone off on other expeditions lasting many years. When he returned, he found to his horror that the 'guardians' had had intercourse with the daughters of men. Naturally they were specially trained men, with all the theoretical and practical knowledge for carrying out their mission, but nevertheless they disobeyed orders by mating! If the 'guardians' altered the natives by manipulating the genetic code, sexual contact – and that is what concerns the Commanding Officer – could have become possible with the second generation of mutated earth-dwellers. As the extra-terrestrial beings were very much older than the beings they met on earth, owing to their different constitution and biological potentialities, they could serve two, three or more of the generations they had reared, before they gave up the oldest leisure game of all. This understandably made the Commanding Officer very angry.

> Chapter 41: I saw the places of the sun and moon, from which they set out and to which they return. Then I saw their wonderful reappearance, how one had precedence over the other, their magnificent path, how they did not step outside the path, did not add to their path, neither take anything away from it . . . Then the invisible and visible way of the moon, and it covers the course of its way in that place by day and by night.

Copernicus wrote his main work *Six Books on the Revolutions of the Celestial Bodies* in 1534. Galileo Galilei discovered the phases of Venus and Jupiter's moon in 1610 with a homemade telescope. The books of both scholars were put on the Index. In 1609 Johannes Kepler discovered the two laws of planetary motion, for which he was the first person to give a dynamic explanation. He started from the assumption that the motions of the planets were caused by a force emitted by the sun. Father Enoch had none of this knowledge!

> Chapter 43: I saw lightning and the stars of heaven, and how they were all named by their names and weighed with a genuine measure, according to the intensity of their light, the breadth of their places and the day of their appearance.

It is a fact that astronomers classify stars by their names and their order of magnitude ('weighed with a genuine measure'), their brightness ('intensity of their light'), their position ('breadth of their places') and the day when they were first observed ('day of their appearance'). Where is this antediluvian prophet supposed to have got these data, if not from the alien cosmonauts?

> Chapter 60: For the thunder has fixed laws for the duration of the clap which is allotted to it. Thunder and lightning are never separated.

As we know, thunder is caused by the sudden expansion of air heated by lightning and moves at the speed of sound (333 metres a second). Thunder *does* have fixed laws 'for the duration of the clap'. How much earlier would natural laws have been discovered if texts like this had not displeased the biblical censors?

> Chapter 69: These are the chiefs of their angels and the names of the leaders of 100, 50 and 10. The name of the first is Jequn; he is the one who seduced the children of the angels, brought them down to earth and made them lust after the daughters of men. The second is called Asbeel; he gave the children of the angels evil counsel so that they defiled their bodies with the daughters of men. The third is called Gadreel: he is the one who showed the children of men all kinds of death-dealing blows. He also showed men the instruments of death, armour, the shield, the broadsword and all kinds of instruments. The fourth is called Penemue: he showed the children of men the difference between good and evil and told them all the secrets of this wisdom. He also taught men how to write with paper and ink. The fifth is called Kasdeya: he taught the children of

men all kinds of blows of spirits and demons, the blows of the embryo in the womb, so that it departs, the serpent's bite, the blows of the noonday heat and the blows of the soul. Enoch recounts the trouble the extraterrestrial beings caused on earth. Children were seduced. The children of men learnt to use murderous weapons. Did Kasdeya teach them methods of abortion ('Blows of the embryo in the womb, so that it departs.')? Did he tell them about psychiatry ('blows of the soul')?

Chapter 72: On that day the sun goes out of the second door and goes down in the west; it returns to the east and rises in the third door on thirty-one mornings and sets in the west of the sky. On that day the night diminishes and consist of nine parts, and the day consists of nine parts, and the night is equal to the day and the year has exactly 364 days. The length of the day and the night, and the shortness of the day and the night, their difference is caused by rotation ... Concerning the small light, which is called moon. In every month its rising and setting are different; its days are like the days of the sun, and when its light is regular, its light amounts to the seventh part of the light of the sun, and in this way it rises ... One half of it projects one seventh, and all the rest of its disc is empty and without light, except for one seventh and one fourteenth of the half of its light ...

On the Commanding Officer's orders, Enoch took down the data literally so that they would be understood in ages to come. In the compendium on astronomy, complicated fractions and exponential series, which are incredibly close to our own mathematical knowledge, cover many pages. Before Enoch disappeared into the cosmos with the gods, he drilled this message into his son:

Chapter 82: And now, my son Methusalem, I tell thee all this and write it down for thee; I have revealed everything to thee and *handed over to thee the books which concern all these things. My son Methusalem, guard these books written by thy father's hand and hand them on to the future generations of the world.*

The Fathers of the Church showed how 'sacred' they considered the order to hand the book down. Were they afraid that the truth would come to light too soon?

1

54

54 In Exodus, Chapter 25, Moses is given exact instructions on how to build the so-called Ark of the Covenant. Moses was warned against making mistakes: 'And look that thou make them after their pattern, which was shewed thee in the mount.' I cannot imagine the Almighty God dragging a chest with him to store his laws in. As a 'model' for this apparatus existed, according to the biblical text, the whole thing must have served a quite different purpose. If the instructions given to Moses are followed, the result is a condenser with a voltage of several hundred volts. And 2 Samuel, 6, tells us about a catastrophe connected with the Ark, which we would immediately diagnose today as an electric shock. When oxen shook the ark, the priest Uzzah took hold of it and fell dead.

Ten short chapters are all that is left of Ezra's writing in the Old Testament. They form the Book of Ezra. Ezra (Hebrew: the help) was a Jewish priest and scribe. In 458 BC he led the Jews out of captivity in Babylon and back to Jerusalem. (The date tallies with Ezekiel's account.) Ezra bound the Jewish community on the Tora, the five Mosaic Books (i.e. the law). In addition to the canonical Book of Ezra there are two apocryphal, rejected books and the fourth Book of Ezra, which was originally written in Hebrew, an apocalypse from the first century AD. It is this fourth book that I am going to write about. It was a victim of the rigorous censorship of the compilers of the Bible.

In the fourth book, the prophet Ezra speaks about the problems of the Jews and indulges in highly futuristic speculations before passing to his real subject, the secret knowledge to which only a select circle had access. At first Ezra claims that he had his 'visions' in bed at night and conversed with 'God' during these visions. If we read about them through modern spectacles, we get a nasty feeling that they were not visions at all. Visions are nearly always illusions of the senses. Too many technical and mathematical details have found their way into these visions. They could not have been dreamt. In the last chapter of the 'forbidden' book Ezra actually reveals that he is talking about real events. He says that he has often met the 'most High' and he was also in the company of his 'angels', who dictated the book to him.

> Assemble the people and say to them that they shall not see thee for forty days. But do thou prepare many writing tablets, take Saraya, Dabria, Selemia, Ethan and Asiel, those five men, for they know how to write quickly, and then come hither . . .
> But when thou hast finished, thou shalt make public the one, but the other thou shalt hand over to the wise men in secret. Tomorrow at this time thou shalt begin to write . . . .
> In this wise ninety-four books were written down in forty days. But when the forty days were over, the most High spoke to me: the twenty-four books that thou hast written first, they shalt thou make public, for the worthy and the unworthy to read; but the last seventy books shalt thou retain and *only hand over to the wise men of thy people.*

So once again there is proof that the so-called gods (cosmonauts) had a definite interest in informing later generations of their presence on earth. *This* particular crew was obviously in a hurry. Perhaps their return launching date had been advanced for unknown technical reasons. Otherwise why were five men who knew how to write quickly summoned to take dictation?

Anyone who would still like to *believe* that the prophet spoke to the great omniscient God (and not to an astronaut) can easily be refuted from the text. 'The most High' freely admits to Ezra that there are some things he himself does not know:

> He answered me and said: the signs about which thou enquirest I can tell thee in part; but about thy life I cannot tell thee, I do not know about it myself.

In conversation with the 'most High' Ezra expatiates on the unrighteousness of this world. As in other holy scriptures, the 'most High' promises that one day he will return from the heavens to take the 'righteous and wise' with him. Return from where? Take the 'righteous and wise' with him whither? To which planet? We can assume that the home planet of the extra-terrestrial spacemen was some light years away from our solar system, because the Commanding Officer (the 'most High') gives Ezra hints about time dilation on interstellar flights at great velocities. Ezra is puzzled; he does not understand (naturally!) and asks the 'most High' if he could not have created all the generations of the past, present and future at one time so that they could all take part in the 'journey home'. Then the following conversation takes place:

> The most High: Ask the womb and say to it: If thou begettest ten children, why dost thou beget each in its time? Challenge it to produce ten at once.
> Ezra: That it cannot do, but only each in its time.
> The most High: Thus have I made the earth into a womb for those who, each in his time, shall be conceived by it. I have established a fixed sequence in the world which I created.

Ezra reflects on these temporal consequences; he wants to know whether the dead or the living will be happier when the return to the heavens takes place. The 'most High' assures him laconically: 'The living are far happier than the dead.'

This lapidary answer is understandable. The Commanding Officer has already told the prophet that the earth is old and 'past the powers of its youth'. According to the laws of time dilation on interstellar flights at high velocities, there is no mystery concealed in this answer, in my view. If the 'most High' returns after some thousands of years have passed, our planet may have become uninhabitable owing to environmental pollution and industrial overexpansion. Those still alive are inhaling the last remnants of oxygen with a death rattle in their throats. It is not surprising that the living whom the 'most High' wants to deport to another planet are by far the 'happier'. The 'most High' tells Ezra that it was he who spoke to Moses and gave him instructions:

> In those days I sent him (Moses) out, I led the people out of Egypt and brought them to Mount Sinai. There I kept him (Moses) with me many days, I told him many wonderful things *and showed him the mysteries of the times.*

There are references to the mystery of the times in many places in the scriptures. In chapter vii, 25, Daniel says that everything will be in the hand of God 'until a time, and times and the dividing of time'. The most High is praised in emphatic words in Psalm xc, 4: 'For a thousand years in thy sight are but as yesterday when it is past, and as a watch in the night.'

Contradictory? Incomprehensible? No. It has long been scientifically proved that entirely different times are applicable on interstellar flights at high velocities. Time on a spaceship travelling just below the speed of light passes much more slowly than on the launching planet where time flies past as usual. Speed and energy can manipulate time. Time dilation was only 'discovered' in our day, but it is a 'law' and has always been valid. So it also applied to the 'gods', who knew all about it. If a spaceship is steadily propelled at one G ($1G = 9.81$ m/sec^2) and braked half way along its course with minus 1G, the following time dilations would take place for the rocket crew and the inhabitants left behind on the earth:

Years for rocket crew	Years for inhabitants of earth
1	1·0
2	2·1
5	6·5
10	24
15	80
20	270
25	910
30	3,100
35	10,600
40	36,000
45	121,000
50	420,000

These tables from Meyer's *Handbook on Space* show that the enormous shifts in time between rocket crew and launching planet have more effect on long journeys. Only 40 brief years pass for the crew of a spaceship propelled at one G, whereas 36,000 years creep by on earth. Once we know this, we can understand why the 'gods' seemed immortal in comparison with men. Is it not possible, according to this law, that the Old Testament prophets, Elijah, Moses and Ezra, whom the gods took with them in a spaceship for their services on earth, are still alive today? We ought to be excited by the idea of their return. There's always room on my agenda for an informative chat with Father Moses! But seriously, just think what we could still find out in the secret libraries!

The fourth book of Ezra ends as follows:

> Then Ezra was carried away and received into the abode of his comrades, after he had written all this down. He is called *the scribe of the knowledge of the most High.*

In the Bodleiean Library, Oxford, there is a manuscript by the Coptic scribe Abu'l Hassan Ma'sudi, catalogued as the Akbar-Ezzeman MS. In it we read:

Surid, a king of Egypt *before the Flood*, had two pyramids built. He ordered his priests to deposit inside them all the wisdom and knowledge of the sciences then available. In the great pyramid they placed information about the heavenly spheres and figures that represent the stars and planets, their positions and cycles, but also the foundations of mathematics and geometry. He did this so that they would be preserved for ever for those descendants who could read the signs.

We are told that King Zoser of the Third Dynasty began to build the step pyramids near Sakkara around 2700 BC. Is the building of the pyramids wrongly dated? Are they incomparably older than archaeologists assume? There is justification for such a suspicion. Abu'l Hassan Ma'sudi is not the only one to assert that the pyramids were built *before the Flood*. Herodotus (484–425 BC), the oldest Greek historian, whom Cicero (106–43 BC) called the 'father of historiography', declares in chapters 141 and 142 of Book II of his *Histories Apodexis* that the priests of Thebes had assured him that the office of high priest had been handed down from father to son for 11,340 years. As proof of this claim, the priests showed Herodotus 341 colossal statues, each of which stood for a high priestly generation. And his hosts assured him that 341 generations ago the gods had lived among men, but that since that time no god had appeared in human form. It is a fact that so far the date of the building of the great pyramids has not been irrefutably proved.

The electronic expert Eric McLuhan, the son of Marshall McLuhan (the Gutenberg Galaxy), stated in Toronto that unknown forces, probably gravitational forces, are still at work in pyramids. In his home at London, Ontario, Canada, he made a red plexiglass pyramid, eighteen inches high, that was a scale-model of the classical pyramids. A simple stand was fixed inside it. On it, roughly in the middle, lay a juicy beefsteak and a razor blade. The steak lay there for twenty days, but it did not go bad or smell. When the razor blade was first deposited, it was blunt from shaving. In two weeks' time it was sharp again. In this simple way McLuhan's collaborators have mummified about 100 eggs and 60lb of steak. These research workers say that anyone can do the same if they build a pyramid with sides and angles corresponding to those of the great pyramid of Gizeh, divide the height of the pyramid by three and place the blunt razor blade exactly in the north-south axis at the height of the bottom third. Plexiglass pyramids with the right dimensions are on sale commercially! (Evering Associates, 43 Eglinton Avenue East, Toronto. Price: 3 dollars.)

With American aid, the University of Cairo built an ultra-sensitive radiation detector connected to a computer inside the Pyramid of Chephren. The detector's job was to register cosmic particles, the computer's to record them. Cosmic particles travelling through hollow spaces reach their goal faster than rays that have to penetrate masonry. The computer supplied incorrect data. The experiment was repeated in 1972. In vain. Dr Amr Gohed, who was in charge of the experiment, told *The Times*: 'Scientifically the thing is impossible. What happens inside the pyramid contradicts all known laws of physics and our electronics!'

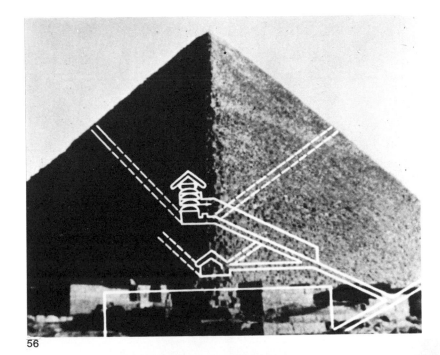

King Rameses II (1290–1224 BC) had two temples built near Abu Simbel, an Upper Egyptian town on the Nile. The larger of the two temples is adorned with four colossal statues of the king that are over sixty feet high. Owing to the construction of the Aswan dam, the temples had to be saved from the rise of the Nile's waters. As the result of an international effort by the western industrial powers organised by UNESCO, temples and statues were raised 180 feet above their original site. The work began in 1964 and was preceded by years of discussion about how to solve the technical problems involved. An array of ultra-modern machines was available, but in spite of that most of the apparatus for transporting the stone giants had to be built *ad hoc*. The statues were cut up into sections, because even the biggest crane in the world could not have lifted them from the ground en bloc, let alone raise them 180 feet into the air. The sawn-up numbered blocks of stone were re-assembled like a gigantic jigsaw puzzle high above the Nile. Anyone who saw the concentration of ultra-modern technical aids during the 'removal' could not help asking himself, 'How on earth did the Ancient Egyptians build these edifices without twentieth-century technology?' Admittedly, at the time the statues were cut out of the living granite on the spot, but how were the statues of Memnon near Thebes that weigh 600 tons transported, or the stone blocks of the terrace at Baalbek, some of which are over 60 feet long and weigh 2,000 tons? And now the sixty-four thousand dollar question: Who nowadays can still accept the 'serious' archaeological explanation that these stone blocks were moved up inclined planes using wooden rollers? The sides of the stones are dressed so accurately that they were fitted together without mortar. There must have been a tremendous amount of waste material on the work sites. Very little has been found. Why did they not build near the granite quarries? I get no answers to questions like that. So could it be true that exterrestrial space travellers helped with their highly developed technology? Yet why did alien spacemen take the trouble? Was it precisely because they wanted to make the children of later millennia ask the questions I dare to ask? (Illustrations 118–119.)

57 Nothing definite is known about this gold figure, which is 2³/₄ inches high. Does it represent Rameses II? But we do know that a sphere on illustrious heads always represents the moon. On the other hand the meaning of the two antenna-like objects is uncertain. Do they symbolise the rulers' previous contact with outer space?

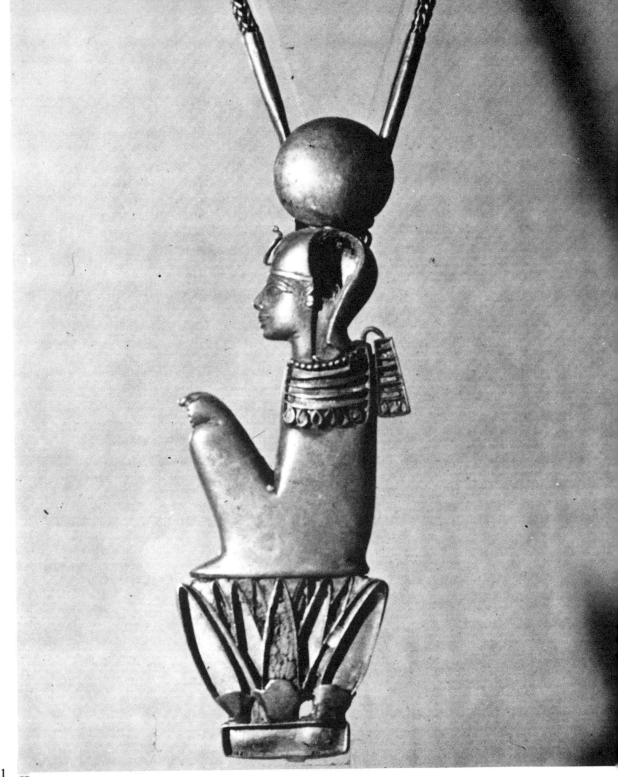

58

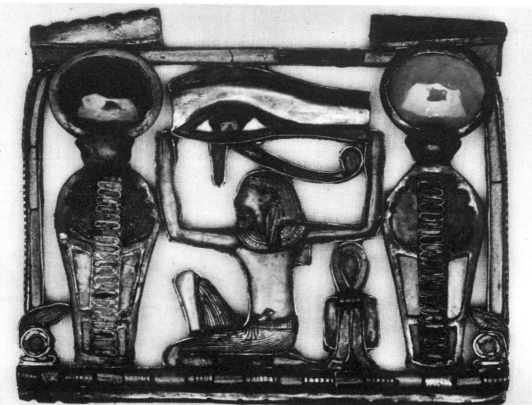

58 Archaeology says that on this chest guardian goddesses of the four cardinal points of the compass support a scarab. I wonder, on the contrary, whether we cannot make out a bowdlerised version of traditional technical knowledge in this and similar works of art.

59 The eye of Horus keeps watch! Once Horus was present, but he vanished into space. His memory is retained in the Ancient Egyptian depictions of his omnipresent far-seeing eye, as shown in this 'Figure of Eternity' from the tomb of Tut-Ankh-Amen.

60 Stele of Naram Sin, 2300 BC. In all ages there has been only one sun. What kind of second sun are these people gazing up at?

60

Professor Dr Herbert Kühn of Mainz wrote: 'Before man discovered writing, he painted his thoughts, his desires and what he implored the godhead for on rocks. These rocks have preserved the primordial speech of mankind right down to our time.' And: 'The surprising thing about the pictures, and what constantly interests us about them, is the fluidity of moulding, the sureness of line, the clarity of configuration, the depth of observation and the skilful grouping of figures with different proportions.' I am in complete agreement with both these basic statements by Professor Kühn, who was one of the first scholars to draw attention to primitive art in his book *The Art of Primitive Peoples*, published in 1923. But our ways part when it comes to his explanations of the content of the rock pictures. Rock paintings, petroglyphs, engravings and reliefs on a rock background have been discovered that date to the Palaeolithic. Here in Central Europe archaeologists have found cave drawings from the Early Palaeolithic, the oldest period in human history, which begins with the emergence of man at the end of the Tertiary and lasts until 10,000 BC. Early Palaeolithic pictures in the form of reliefs have been found in the open, whereas most of the outdoor paintings and engravings that have been found date only to the post-Palaeolithic. East Spain, South Africa and Siberia possess the oldest rock drawings from the Middle Palaeolithic. More numerous are the finds from the Neolithic and the Bronze and Iron Ages, which date however to the second and first millennia BC. Henri Lhote, who investigated the rock paintings of the Sahara, is convinced that the oldest were executed between 8000 and 6000 BC. Incredible works of art are to be found in almost inaccessible places – in remote caves during the Ice Age, later on the highest ridges of mountains where people scarcely ever went. Paleolithic artists painted and engraved all over the world. The paintings were executed with brushes and stubs, and look as if they had been done today. Minerals (ochre, manganese dioxide and feldspar) and charcoal were used as colours. The commonest colour is red, followed by black and white. During the Palaeolithic, engravings were hammered or scratched with flint tools. But in both engravings and paintings the same motifs constantly recur, gods with haloes and helmets, gods with clothes like the overall suits of modern astronauts, gods with accessories which *we* can easily recognise as antennae. If these were individual cases within a radius of 1,000 or 3,000 miles, they might be coincidences and we should have to accept them without comment. Yet we find the selfsame motifs on all continents, in France, Italy and America, in Southern Rhodesia and Peru, in Chile, Mexico, Brazil and Australia, in Russia and in the Sahara. I have read the explanations of the sense and meaning of the pictures assiduously. The explanations satisfy neither my thirst for knowledge nor my intellect. As if I was in a religion class at school, I feel that I *ought to believe* explanations that don't convince me. We are told that we *must* see and understand things in a certain way, because we *ought* not to interpret them differently. Why *must* we? Why *oughtn't* we? 'Undoubtedly there was a parallel development between the various palaeolithic, Mesolithic and Neolithic stages in India, Europe and Africa,' writes Marcel Brion in *The Early Civilisations of the World*. Undoubtedly, but how did it happen? Scholars say the prehistoric painters painted after nature. I don't deny they had seen the animals they depicted. But where did these Palaeolithic naturalistic artists, whose studios were somewhere in the Sahara, get the models for the floating beings in spacesuits with modern zip-fasteners and broad bands at their wrists? Naturalistic painters copy nature; they have virtually no imagination. Another theory is that the paintings should be interpreted psychologically. The cave painters ate sacred mushrooms, fell into a trance and saw their surrealistic visions while drugged. When they came to their senses, they scratched the fantastic figures on the walls. I am afraid these explanations are more indefensible than my speculations. I think in more practical terms. I do not bother about depth psychology. I say to myself that if a cavedweller, even though clad in skins, portrayed figures in unfamiliar suits, with helmets on their heads, he must have seen such beings. No drugs; no imagination; no manikins. No models; no naturalism. Yet another theory is that the rock paintings represent ritual emblems and hunting scenes. A reasonable explanation as long as others are not excluded. It is simply unscientific to say that there is no reason for prehistorians to envisage the former presence of extra-terrestrial beings during the history of mankind's development.

A discipline, whatever its subject, should try to get as close as possible to the truth. It can only do so if it submits its doubtful positions to discussion and includes the originally unthinkable in its investigations. I am reproached for ignoring 'accepted facts' in the sphere of prehistory. What kind of 'facts' are they? Every newly discovered rock painting is 'interpreted' just long enough for it to be fitted into the standard framework. There are no accurate datings, because charcoal and bone remains found in caves do not imply that they necessarily date to the time of the cave paintings. Up till now all datings are putative. Once prehistorians and archaeologists accept the demonstrable presence of a spaceship around 593 BC (Ezekiel!), light will be thrown on the darkness enshrouding the rock paintings with the selfsame motifs found all over the world. Alien cosmonauts were in contact with the men of their period all round the globe. They were seen, observed and portrayed by Palaeolithic men. Henri Lhote, who discovered the figure of a man nearly 18 feet high in a rocky gorge in the Sahara, wrote:

> The outlines are simple and crude; the round head, in which the only peculiarity is the double oval in the middle of the face, is reminiscent of the image we usually form of Martians. Martians!...
> If 'Martians' really visited the Sahara, it must have been thousands of years ago, for as far as we know, the portraits of the roundheads at Tassili are very, very old.

Now let the pictures speak for themselves.

61 Henri Lhote discovered a whole art gallery of figures looking like astronauts in the Tassili Mountains (Sahara). Note the reinforcing bands at knees and elbows, the diagonal bands around the chest, as well as the belts and helmets.

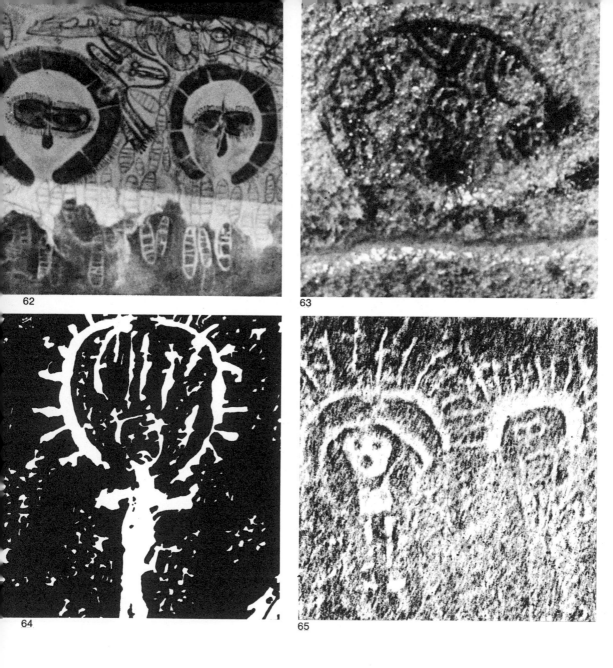

62   In the Kimberley Range in Australia . . .

63   In the Tassili Mountains in the Sahara . . .

64   Near Fergana in Russia . . .

65   On the plain of Nazca, Peru . . .

66 67

68 69

66–67   In the Sahara (the 'Great Martian God', right in the original, left clarified by white lines) . . .

68   On a rock-drawing in the vicinity . . .

69   . . . and in Val Camonica, Italy, we find rock-drawings that are strikingly similar in spite of the thousands of miles that separate them, and each one of them could have inspired Henri Lhote to invent the name 'Great Martian God'.

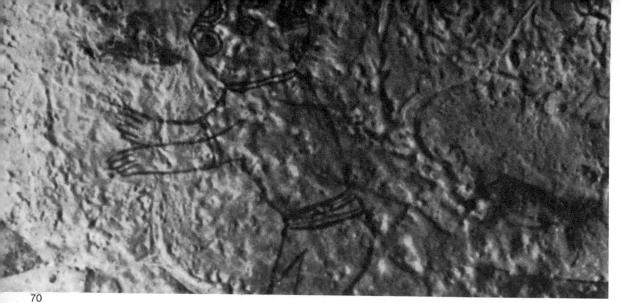

70

71

70–71 This astronaut on the rock face in the Tassili Mountains and the astronautical event in a rock painting near Fergana are explained 'psychologically' or interpreted as 'taken from Nature'. What familiar natural objects did the eyes that watched the first astronauts and the first journey to the moon recognise?

72 The 'Star-blower', a petroglyph by the Hopi Indians.

72

The hunting grounds of the Hopi Indians, members of the large Pueblo group, are located in Arizona and New Mexico. The Hopis, who number about 8,000 today, preserve ancient rites and customs and oral traditions on their reserves, where ancient rock drawings also abound. The present chief of the tribe, White Bear, can still interpret most of them. As similar drawings can be found all over the world, White Bear's knowledge might be very useful in helping to explain the hitherto inexplicable, but the chief will not reveal his secret. It is exclusively preserved and handed down in the inmost circles of the tribe. The Hopi legend says that their ancestors came from 'endless space' and had visited various worlds before they reached earth. If we accept the Hopi traditions, all the red rock drawings we come across are no more than very early signposts left by members of the tribe who passed through the region at some time and left information for subsequent generations.

73

74

73 A two-colour rock painting from New Zealand. Note the cluster of rays that shoot from the head. The connection of the terrestrial and the celestial was depicted like that from time immemorial.

74. Primordial Australian gods, called the 'Two creative beings'.
Note the boxes fastened to the chest with straps.

75

76

75 'Has the deadly breath of the heavenly beast smitten you?' Gilgamesh asks his friend Enkidu. We read in the Indian Mahabharata that everything was struck 'by the poisonous breath of the god'. Did the Stone Age artist who made this rock drawing near Navoy, Russia, know about such an event? Is that why he equipped the beings within range of the deity's deadly poisonous breath with gas masks?

76 This is how the Australian aborigines represent their earliest gods – in this case on a rock near Port Headland.

77 Uninterpreted rock relief with a sun and concentric circles near Paraiba, Brazil.

78 Unknown star constellation on a stone engraving near Lagoa Santa (Minas Gerais, Brazil).

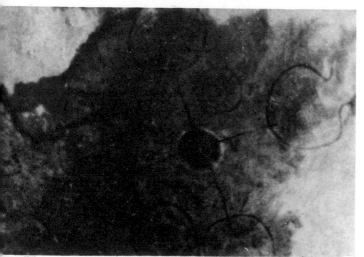

79 Inexplicable objects in a rock drawing from Tassili, Sahara.

80 Flying object on a rock near Sete Cidades, Brazil.

80

81 Near Goiania, Brazil. Note the delicate engraving. A god with a crown of rays.

81

82 The Indians from Sete Cidades also stylised stars, which they could only see as spots of light with the bare eye.

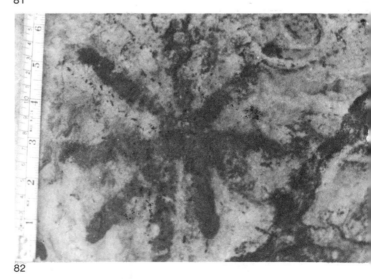

82

83

83–84 The Pedra de Gávea lies to the south of Rio de Janeiro. Every tourist can recognise the head and body of a sphinx in the top of the mountain. Like other sphinxes, this one too is mysterious. Serious scholars say that the outlines of the sphinx were caused by natural erosion, that is that the strange figure was a freak of nature. Other equally serious scholars say that it was artificially carved out of the mountain top. They base their view on the fact that letters identified by the American Professor Cyrus Gordon as Phoenician characters line the contours of the sphinx's body. On two occasions I flew round the Pedra de Gávea in an army helicopter. I landed on the summit and stood on the plateau with the seven incised circles. I could not make up my mind which explanation was correct. But other finds on and around this mountain would inevitably be disconcerting.

86

87

85 This giant's foot, discovered by Eduardo Chaves, has been lying in the undergrowth at Pedra de Gavea for thousands of years. My friend Eduardo has been tracking down curiosities in the mountains round Rio de Janeiro for years.
For those who are interested, his address is: Caixa Postal 24056 – ZC – 09, 20.000 Rio de Janeiro – Guonabora.

86–87 No-one now claims that these mysterious petroglyphs originated from natural causes. To whom were they supposed to give a message? To whom *did* they give a message? Were they signals or communications to extraterrestrial beings?

88

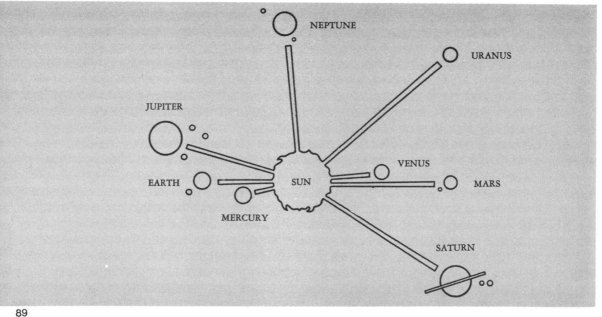

NEPTUNE

URANUS

JUPITER

VENUS

EARTH

SUN

MARS

MERCURY

SATURN

89

88–89 An extraordinary rock drawing was discovered in the caves of Varzelandia, Brazil. Eight of the nine planets in our system are drawn in their correct relations to the sun – proof of astronomical knowledge that Stone Age artists just did not have. Who were their teachers?

90–91 Gigantic stone heads of robots in the Olmec Park at Villahermosa, Mexico.

90

92

93

I have asked several philologists where the word god comes from. When my learned friends tracked it back through Hebrew and Aramaic texts to very early periods, they told me that in the very earliest writings the singular 'god' did not exist. The first mythological traditions spoke exclusively in the plural of 'the gods', and this primordial concept was roughly translatable as 'those

94

94 A picture of a god from the late Paracas period, Peru.

circling in the clouds'. Who circled in the clouds in antiquity? Why do the questions of man's origin and descent continue to excite such passion? Because the previous answers were unconvincing, because they stretched our credulity instead of enlightening us. It does not get us any further forward to know that god or the gods worried about the trivial daily cares of our ancestors, so long as god or the gods remain the omnipotent omniscient phenomena we have always been told about. If they only visited the earth for short periods, but were not real beings, how could they, as is reported, have instructed our forefathers in the practice of agriculture and given them formulas for the production and working of metal? If god or gods were never visible, how did their pictures originate? Could primitive peoples portray something they had not seen? How could they represent unimaginable beings figuratively? Was it eagerness to encounter the unimaginable that ultimately drove them to create their likenesses from phantasmagoria? I hardly think so, because even in the earliest portrayals, the gods look very much like humans. Did prehistoric man take his own or his neighbour's (stylised) image for 'god'? He experienced birth and death, but the gods were immortal to him. Fantasy gods, which they would necessarily have been in that case, would not have remained in his consciousness for thousands of years. No, 'those circling in the clouds' were temporary visitors from other stars. That would supply a plausible explanation of why cultures and civilisations everywhere developed in leaps and bounds at intervals of thousands of years. I agree with Teilhard de Chardin when he says that the religion of tomorrow could be a beautiful thing and that it should put its trust in science.

95

96

97

98

95–97 In archaeology these three pre-historic figurines are known as 'Man with Catfish Head', the 'Venus of Willendorf' and 'Fourfaced Sun Symbol'. All three are accepted as mother goddesses, are more than 10,000 years old and symbolise the origin of intelligence. The deformed heads – akin to the rock drawings – indicate a non-human origin.

98 This stylisation of a representation from the Museum für Völkerkunder, Hamburg, shows an Indian in contact with a flying dragon. The robot-like objects that lurk in the background occur in myths as 'beings who neither eat meal, nor drink water'.

Eduardo Jensen, a general in the Chilean Air Force, has astonished archaeologists on more than one occasion during the last few years. An active pilot, he has taken photographs of figures on the mountainsides of Chile. From Mollende in Peru down to the Chilean province of Antofagasta, he found gigantic markings on the sheer slopes, circles with rays directed inwards, ovals filled with chessboard patterns, rectangles and arrows. At a height of 300 feet above the desert of Taratacar in northern Chile, one can see the stylised figure of a man, a robot. The creature is rectangular, with straight legs and a square head sitting on a thin neck. Twelve antennae emerge from its head. Flying fins are attached to the body on both sides ending at the rump. The general has also discovered another prehistoric figure, which is over 365 feet high. I reproduce it in the illustration below. The arms are bent, a little monkey seems to cling to its left elbow. A slightly bent staff that broadens towards the end grows from its left shoulder. What is the purpose, meaning and age of this figure? Question marks. For the time being archaeologists have catalogued it as a 'religious symbol'. It's a bit big, situated *rather* high up and it's *very* remote. So who was supposed to see the robot?

99

100

101

100, 101, 103 These Mayan reliefs in Mexico are known as 'Bee gods'. I cannot make out any connection with bees. Beings lie on their stomachs with arms bent and the most likely object to put in their hands would be a control-column. The feet, which are shod, (103), rest on stilt-like sprung legs with large supporting discs at the end.

102 The stele of Santa Lucia, Cotzmal-huapa, Guatemala, shows (below right) a figure who is dressed like a modern space traveller. Above a 'Bee god' supports himself on the sun!

The Yucatan peninsula lies between the Gulf of Campeche and the Caribbean Sea in Central America. After the Spanish conquest, Bishop Diego de Landa organised a gigantic auto-da-fe in the town of Mani in 1672. An unknown number of ancient Maya manuscripts were burnt – an irreplaceable cultural treasure. In chapter 41 of his book *Relación de la cosas de Yucatan,* Bishop Landa boasts about this infamous act:

> We found many books with their characters and drawings, but they contained nothing but superstition, lies and evil. So we burnt them all, which they deplored and which obviously wounded them deeply.

One Maya legend says that there was a civilisation in full flower 10,000 years ago. Although archaeologists question this early dating in their meagre 'revelations', I shall continue to attach great importance to it, seeing that no-one can even explain where the Maya came from or where they went to. For it has been proved that the Maya cities were not destroyed by wars or natural catastrophes, they were simply abandoned by their inhabitants. The Maya disappeared without a trace. Why did they leave their magnificent cities, which were built 'to last' with massive blocks of stone? It is *proved* that the so-called pre-classical period stretched back into the second millennium BC, but, and scholars admit this, they know virtually nothing about the actual archaic period which preceded the pre-classical one. It is highly probable that all the historical facts missing today were in the books that Bishop de Landa burnt. Only three Maya manuscripts, the so-called Codices, were spared in the burning of the books. They were prepared from the bark of fig-trees and folded

102

103

like a concertina. These fragments are named after the places where they are now kept: the Codex Dresdensis, the Paris Codex and the Madrid Codex, also known as Tro-Cortesianus. The glyphs, whose colours are yellowed with age, are still virtually uninterpreted. What has been deciphered is their brilliant but simple numerical system. They counted in dashes with dots on top. One dot equals 1, three dots equal 3, etc. The figure 5 was expressed by a dash, so that 7 becomes a dash with two dots above it. The figure 17 consists of three dashes and two dots. The Maya even knew about relative values and zero. They used the vigesimal system, based on twenty. If they wanted to write 23, they put three dots in the unit place and one dash in the twenties place. It was easy to distinguish the twenties dash from a five dash. The dashes standing for higher values were placed a considerable distance above the dashes representing five. The Maya calendar was of an incredibly high calibre. The date for the start of their chronology was a day in the year 3113 BC. South American experts claim that the mysterious year 3113 has no connection with the actual history of the Maya, but has a purely 'symbolic' value, like the Jewish phrase 'since the creation of the world'. How can they say that with absolute certainty, when we do not know where the Maya came from or where they vanished to? A great deal has been written about the Maya calendar. One fact is that it operated with cycles of years that were only supposed to have repeated themselves every 374,000 years. Edifices were built according to the calendar: for each day of the month a step, for each month a platform, and at the top, on the 365th day, rose the temple. It almost looks as if the Maya of the ancient kingdom did not build their temples because they were impelled by religious zeal, but because the calendar imposed on them a duty they had to fulfil. The astronomers' observatory, a round building on top of two enormous terraces, which towered up high above the virgin forest, was located at Chichen Itza. The Maya astronomers knew the moon's orbit to four decimal places and they could even calculate the Venusian year to three decimal places. The Mayas' primordial gods came from the stars, communicated with the stars and returned to them, according to legend. The *Popol Vuh*, the creation myth of the Quiché Maya, relates that 400 heavenly youths returned to the Pleiades after fighting with men and suffering degradation. The god Kukulkan presumably corresponds to the Aztec god Quetzalcoatl. He was depicted as a feathered serpent and came from the stars. As the Maya saw snakes wriggling along the ground every day of their lives, it is difficult to understand why the snakes in drawings and reliefs could *fly*. The Mayan manuscripts still extant cover 208 pages folded concertina-fashion. Given the multiplicity of signs, figures, emblems and the resulting possible combinations of them, it is not surprising that so little has been deciphered to date. The drawings on fig-tree fibre, with a thin layer of chalk as a foundation for the paint, are preserved between sheets of glass. The Dresden Codex has 74 pages and contains astronomical calculations, as well as tables of the movements of the Moon and Venus. A snakelike monster constantly appears in the heavens next to the numerals. It is connected with the moon and spews water on to the earth. The beings wear complicated headgear and masks, and often seem to be wearing a kind of diving-suit. Are they Maya priests performing experiments on animals? Indefinable figures with peculiar implements abound. The Paris Codex was bought from a private collection by the Bibliothèque Nationale in 1832. It is made of the same material and has 22 badly damaged, painted pages. The preservation of the folding pages was so careless in the last century that only two pages of the treasure, which is kept in a glass casket, are now on show. Luckily for us there are reproductions made in 1887. The Paris Codex mainly contains calendar prophecies. The Madrid Codex is housed in the Museo de America and consists of 112 illuminated pages, on which gods in grotesque ritual positions can be seen. The pictures and their details are fascinating. One could read all kinds of things into them. Smoking gods on the glyph of the earth, gods before eating vessels, punishment by piercing the tongue, a goddess with a snake's head at the spinning-wheel. I reproduce parts of the Codices, which are vitually unknown except to experts, so that *unprejudiced* observers can judge what is *really* portrayed. I am assuming that the layman will formulate ideas more freely than the Maya specialist (see coloured plates).

During his researches in the field from 1949 to 1952, the Mexican archaeologist Alberto Ruz Lhuiller discovered a burial chamber in the Temple of the Inscriptions at Palenque. From the ante-room of the temple, which lies on the highest platform of a stepped pyramid, a steep flight of steps, slippery with moisture, leads down nearly 75 feet and ends six feet underground. The steps were concealed in such a way that they must have been deliberately kept secret. The dimensions and situation of the chamber correspond to 'magical or symbolical conceptions' (Marcel Brion). It took archaeologists and their helpers three years to clear the way from the top to the bottom of the steps. The floor of the chamber was formed by a monolith 14 feet long by 7 feet broad, with an extraordinary stone bas-relief. I do not know another relief of such beauty and precision. Maya glyphs are engraved round the edges of the tablet, but very few of them have been deciphered. The stone plaque is decorated with glyphs of the kind we know from Maya literature (Codices!) and steles. We find the tree of life (or cross of life), an Indian wearing the mask of the earth god, with feathered ornaments on his chest, small jade tubes and cords, and last but not least the sacred Quetzal bird, a two-headed snake and symbolical masks. The archaeologist Paul Rivet, one of the experts on this find, says that the Indian is depicted sitting on the sacrificial altar and that 'stylised beard hair of the weather god' is engraved behind his seat, recurrent motifs in Maya cities. Beneath this nobly decorated monolith a skeleton in a coffin painted scarlet was found. A gold mask covered its face; some jade jewellery was laid beside the skeleton, as were ritual objects and sacrificial gifts.

Ever since I saw the tombstone at Palenque, I have interpreted it in technical terms. It makes no difference whether you look at it sideways or lengthways – the feeling that it is a space traveller haunts you. The best photos (known to me) of the tombstone, which lies behind a locked iron grille, were taken by the camera-men of the film *Chariots of the Gods*. After we had made eight applications, the government allowed us to work for half an hour with camera and searchlights. These pictures will give the

104

105

reader a better idea of what I am talking about than the ones in
my first book. Altogether the tombstone forms a frame in the
middle of which a being is sitting and leaning forwards (like an
astronaut in his command module). This strange being wears a
helmet from which twin tubes run backwards. In front of his
nose is an oxygen apparatus. The figure is manipulating some
kind of controls with both hands. The fingers of the upper hand
are arranged as if the being was making a delicate adjustment to
a knob in front of him. We can see four fingers of the lower hand,
which has its back to us. The little finger is crooked. Doesn't
it look as if the being were working a control such as the hand-
throttle of a motor-bike? The heel of the left foot rests on a pedal
with several steps. The observer of the Palenque relief will be
struck by the fact that the 'Indian on the Sacrificial Altar' is
dressed in a very modern way. Just below his chin is a kind of
rollneck pullover. The tightly fitting upper part of his suit ends
at the wrists in turned back cuffs. He wears a broad belt with a
safety fastening round his waist, trousers with a wide mesh
pattern and tight socklike garments down to the ankles – the

perfect outfit for an astronaut! In my view, the apparatus in which the space traveller crouches so tensely, presents the following technical characteristics. The central oxygen machine lies in front of the strapped-in astronaut, as do the energy supply and communications system, not to mention the manual controls and equipment for observations outside the spacecraft. In the bow of the ship, i.e. ahead of the central unit, large magnets are recognisable. Presumably their purpose was to create a magnetic field around the ship's hull that would prevent it from being struck by particles when travelling at high speeds in outer space. Behind the astronaut we can see a nuclear fusion unit. Two atomic nuclei, probably hydrogen and helium, which finally merge, are schematically depicted. I find it important that the rocket exhaust is shown in stylised form at the end of the spaceship *outside* the frame. Of course, there are also recurrent Maya glyphs on the tombstone *in addition to* these technically interpreted features. To me it is self-evident that the Maya supplied news about their 'celestial messenger' and inscribed his history in a way familiar to them. After the sojourn of an extraterrestrial being, the Indians naturally wished to perpetuate his exalted visit and the spacecraft itself in a relief. But apart from the fact that the stonemasons would not have had the technical knowledge, it would have been impossible to chisel in stone an apparatus as complicated as this one-man spaceship simply from personal observation. Did they ask their heavenly visitors for advice? Did the extraterrestrial spacemen give the Maya artists a simplified schematic drawing of a spaceship? To the sceptic who asks me why the spacemen should have revealed their knowledge and secrets, I can only answer that they did so in this case, as on other occasions, to leave behind visible evidence of their presence for later generations.

Once this speculation is accepted, the presence of partially deciphered glyphs does not exclude the coexistence of a technical explanation. There is no definitive proof that we are dealing with the usual Maya symbolism on this tombstone. We cannot irrefutably deduce from the literature that the relief contains no technical elements. It does not get us much further if we stand to attention in front of antiquated working hypotheses.

108, 109, 110 It is well-known that snakes have never been able to fly. Yet to give only two examples that are continents apart, I show a flying snake from the temple at Uxmal, Mexico, and another from the Valley of the Kings, Egypt. On this subject Robert Charroux quotes the historian Sanchuniaton (1250 BC): 'The snake has a speed that nothing can exceed because of its breath . . . its energy is exceptional . . . it has illuminated everything with its gleam . . .' That is not a description of the usual snakes men saw wriggling about on the earth! Surely they were really meant to portray beings with astronautical equipment, like the one on the ancient vase in San Salvador (110)? Stylisation can very quickly change such a being into a snake!

Archaeologists refuse to include a knowledge of spacetravel technology in their discipline, so it seems intolerant of them to reject my version. A stalemate should be agreed on. The tombstone cannot be satisfactorily explained by the Maya literature and the technical version is conceivable.

I do not know whether the UN or some other well-endowed international organisation has issued statistics on how many thousands of square yards of ground are dug up daily in regions rich in cultural relics to make cities, roads, industries, airports and sportsgrounds. But I am quite certain that no archaeological investigation of these sites is made. No prehistorian, no engineer with an interest in prehistory or archaeologist is present. I am convinced that we should not be groping so helplessly in the darkness of our remote past if the interior of the earth was examined. When colonisers began to conquer new continents centuries ago, they gave the natives presents such as glass beads, mirrors and cloth. And if they wanted to curry favour with a chieftain or a whole tribe, they produced the more valuable items such as knives, axes, nails, saws, and cooking pots for the women. Is it too far-fetched to imagine that alien cosmonauts also gave our ancestors presents in the form of tools during their visits to earth? I know that no tools of extraterrestrial origin have been found so far. Indeed, they cannot have been found, because they have never been looked for. Have we at least an approximate idea of what these tools could or ought to look like? No, we haven't, but remember this. In our grandfathers' day radios were still clumsy wooden boxes, with loudspeakers big enough to put a child's head it. *Today* transmitter and receiver can be fitted into a miniset the size of a pea and the loudspeaker is one third the size of a matchbox. What I am trying to say is that the end products of technology require less and less room. The tools of highly industrialised extraterrestrial beings would not necessarily be big or strong enough to withstand bulldozers and pickaxes. Are we thoughtlessly trampling on valuable artefacts?

111   Above the Inca fortress of Sacsayhuaman, Peru, there are several places where the rock has been worked in the most incredible way. I asked people on the spot (South American scholars for preference) what they meant and what technical aids had been used to make them. The answer? No-one knows who worked here, when they worked or what tools they used. But no-one is rash enough to claim that Nature was responsible!

112

113

114

115

116

117

112–117   I took all these photos on the mountain slopes above Sacsayhuaman. Scholars say that everything in them was the result of glaciation (112). But if you examine the terrain closely – and I spent weeks
up there – the stone puzzles really hit you in the eye. Sections cut out
of the rock with right-angled edges and polished surfaces (113); inexplicable bath-tub-like depressions (114); right-angled wedges in the
rock (115) that seem meaningless today; stone show-cases cut out as if
by a cheeseknife (116), and last but not least thrones for giants (117).
What does it all mean?

118

119

Cuzco lies 11,370 feet above sea-level. Not far from this Peruvian town lies the Inca fortress of Sacsayhuaman, a tourist attraction of the first rank. It impresses the visitor with its monolithic blocks, which weigh more than 100 tons. The sides of the blocks are so smooth that Robert Charroux suspects that they must have been subjected to chemical treatment. But what fascinates me most is not that, nor the three ramparts of squared blocks 18 feet high, nor the terrace wall over 1,500 feet long and 55 feet high. My wonderland lies just over half a mile away at a height of 11,480 to 12,415 feet. I clambered up to the platform over crevasses and deep holes in the rock. In the rarefied atmosphere which makes it difficult to breathe, you are not expecting anything else after the marvels below, but suddenly you are confronted with neatly cut stone monsters. One of the examples I measured with rectangular sides was 7 feet by 11 feet 1 inch by 2 feet 8 inches. It was cut out of a lump of stone 33 feet high and 54 feet wide. There was also a concrete block 39 feet high, polished and ground as if it had just been delivered by the mason. Of course, it is not concrete; the stone is granite worked with the utmost skill. I squeezed myself into niches in the rock. I found the same accurate workmanship everywhere. Where is the debris left by the craftsmen? There should be chippings somewhere, because the clefts are too narrow for them to have been taken away. I agree with Charroux' opinion, but I am also convinced that an explosion took place up here that shifted the rocks and caused the stone to melt. I climbed down into a cave nearly 240 feet deep. Shaken by some primaeval force, its straight downward course is interrupted in several places, but parts of the walls and ceiling have survived the catastrophe. Outside masses of rock that has been split in pieces are scattered about right down into the valley of the Urubamba. They were parts of a whole and show signs of the most accurate workmanship, yet they can never again be reintegrated into a master plan. I asked experts in Cuzco and Lima about the meaning and origin of these formations. No one could say anything definite. That is nothing to be ashamed of. But to sum up: the whole complex above Sacsayhuaman was erected by methods unknown to us at some unknown date, and it already existed when the sons of the sun built the Inca fortress. I am reproached for constantly attacking the world of scholarship. Am I really

01

120

121

122

120–125 These stoneworks, which no-one has explained so far, can be seen on the mountainsides, about 5,900 feet above sea-level, above Cuzco, Peru. You can run your hands over beautifully polished surface areas (120); you would say that the wooden mould had just been removed from cast concrete (121). Yet in spite of the masterly workmanship it is not concrete, but accurately worked granite. What can have been the purpose of these neatly executed works in rocky gorges (122)? If you want to stimulate your own particular fancy, take a good look at the detailed photos (123–125). Surely a new way of looking at things is needed up here at the world's end?

123

124

125

doing so? Actually I am striving to lure them to the sites of the unsolved mysteries of the world.

I have carried out detailed research work at Tiahuanaco on two occasions. The last time I set out from Cuzco, Peru, and travelled all day by rail and boat to reach the little village 12,000 feet above sea-level on the Bolivian plateau. The little railway station would certainly have very few customers, had not the site become famous for its stone mysteries. The 'museum' lies just behind the station – a series of puzzles that stand only fifteen feet from the railway viaduct. They consist of neatly polished rectangular stones with dead straight grooves the thickness of a finger, worked with great precision as if each piece had a counterpart into which it must fit. Were the builders working on the manufacture of standardised units? What plans were they following? The grooves all run at right angles to the surface area. One cannot argue about objects with grooves running round the stone, but it is curious when rectangular pieces are 'pinched' out of the stone and the grooves run parallel to the surface area. These grooves could not have been made with any tools that we credit the Incas with. They have been milled. But how? Even a modern groove milling machine could only make such grooves with very small mills rotating at high speeds. The monoliths at Tiahuanaco also exhibit similar grooves that run from top to bottom and obviously the idea was that they should be fitted together with other monoliths. In a reconstructed temple eager restorers have stacked rectangular stones between the monoliths, which now form a wall. The grooves in the monoliths have been concealed by this addition and essential evidence of the *genuine, technical* Tiahuanaco has vanished. Problems are not solved like that! Sections of stone conduits protrude from these walls at right angles. What are they doing in the wall? Were they intended to catch rainwater? There are no side conduits. I dug up some pieces in the shape of the half-section of a pipe. Both the right-angled and the straight sections usually had the *lower half* missing. Nevertheless, I read that the 'pipes' were water conduits.

127 The monolithic Gate of the Sun at Tihuanaco is 9 feet high and 12 feet wide. On it three rows of 48 squares containing figures flank a flying god. The weight of the Gate of the Sun has been worked out at ten tons. I suspect that here too the remains of technical know-how were handed down in these reliefs. The facts that they have not yet been interpreted in no way invalidates my suspicion.

TIAHUANACO

126

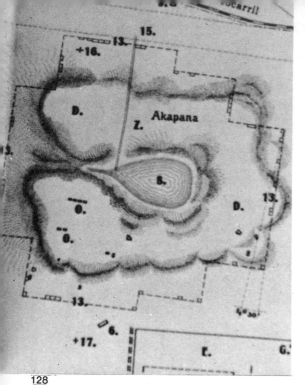

128

129

128 The dried-out pond at Akapana shows that Tiahuanaco was once connected with Lake Titicaca. The same sediments as at Lake Titicaca are found on its muddy verges, with their scanty fauna. Today Lake Titicaca lies several miles from the ruins of Tiahuanaco. This change in the topography, which was the work of many, many millennia, shows the legendary age of Tiahuanaco.

129–132 These four photos, which I took at Tiahuanaco, will support the remarks I have made in the text about these so-called water conduits!

130

In all ages the lower halves of water conduits would surely have been more important than the upper halves? In one example, 3 feet 8 inches long, I found two parallel half-pipes without the lower halves! If the pre-Inca engineer decided that the pipe did not carry enough water, why didn't he enlarge the *existing* groove? Why, in the name of all the Inca gods, did he carve a second half-pipe only two centimetres away? If the missing lower halves alone suggest that these were no water conduits, the double parallel pipes seem to me to refute the idea absolutely. The mysterious world of Tiahuanaco has been archaeologically dated from bone and charcoal remains. It is assumed that the buildings originated around 600 BC. An ideal date! The prophet Ezekiel's encounter with a spaceship took place in 592 BC. Is it not conceivable that the extraterrestrial spacemen set up a base at Tiahuanaco? The ground crew stayed on our planet for twenty years, as J. Blumrich, the NASA engineer, has shown. The astronauts did not bring building materials with them, but they possessed tools with which the material on the spot could have been suitably worked. *This* interpretation would solve many puzzles. The strangers departed, leaving behind the monolithic structures. The Aymaras, the Indian civilisation the structures are attributed to, transformed the functions of the edifices for their own purposes. Only then was the temple built and rectangular wall components placed between the monoliths. What has been reconstructed today is simply the past of the Aymaras, not that of the original builders, who ran power cables through the pipes under extraterrestrial guidance.

131

132

133

134

If we followed the Aztec calendar, the present age is ripe for the destruction of the earth by an earthquake. During construction work in Mexico in 1790, a round stone disc 3 feet thick and 12 feet in diameter was found. A bas-relief of faces, arrows and circles was carved on the stone. It was soon discovered that these motifs were data for a calendar, the secret Aztec calendar. But the Aztecs themselves were not the 'inventors' of this fantastic calendar, they took over essential parts of it from their forefathers, the Maya. In the centre is the head of the Sun God, in a closed ring surrounded by twenty identical squares, in which the twenty symbols of the 260-day Maya calendar, known as the Tzolkin, are inscribed. There is a different symbol applicable to each day and all the symbols together give the four 'great ages'. The calendar relates that in the dim past jaguars came and destroyed the prehistoric animals, after which storms carried men away. In the third age there was rain of fire and a global flood. Oh yes, and the present age, called '4 Olin', is going to be wiped out by an earthquake.

133–134 These mono-liths at Tiahuanaco are still more stone documents showing pre-historic precision work.

136

137

The gods stand on a platform at Tula, Mexico. The legend has it that this was the place where the lower gods were in contact with the higher gods. The partners were in communication by cords. The lower gods received 'flashes of lightning' from the higher gods; finally they set out to punish ungrateful men. At Cocha, Peru, the gods were so wrathful that they melted the rocks on which men lived with their divine lightning.

The statues of the gods at Tula have noble heads with deeply incised eyes. But what are those stiff ear protectors? What sort of boxes have they on their chests? Didn't the moon astronauts carry very similar apparatuses on *their* chests? What have they got in their hands? Archaeologists say that they are 'symbolical keys'. Keys to what? Perhaps the legends are right after all. What else can be held in two fingers if not ray-guns, laser appliances, which melted the rocks by the emission of radiation. Engineers of the world, unite!

138

139

140

142

142 Like all the pyramids at Teotihuacan, Mexico, the sun pyramid, too, is aligned according to the stars. The oldest text about the site tells that the gods assembled here and took council about man, even before *homo sapiens* existed.

Ancient man always sought the gods in the mountains. Up there he wanted to be near them, there he wanted to observe them, experience their arrival and record their disappearance into the sky. In low countries where there are no mountains, our ancestors built artificial mountains. What else is the Tower of Babel if not an observation post? Are not the pyramids steps that take man nearer to the gods?

The pyramid near Santa Cruz in Bolivia presents a special problem. It is a fairly symmetrical, apparently artificial mountain. Two deep bored grooves like launching ramps run from the bottom to the top of this mountain and end suddenly in mid-air.

The Indians in the valley tell each other legends which recount that their gods ascended into heaven on 'fiery horses' on these two grooves.

For once the archaeologists have no explanation of this.

143

The ruins of Baalbek are located in the Lebanon, on the Beirut-Homs railway line and road, at a height of 3,760 feet. In the first and second centuries AD, the Roman Emperor Augustus had magnificent temples, the ruins of which are admired by tourists from all over the world, built on the site of ruins left by the Greeks. In reality, the marvel and mystery of Baalbek is not of Greek or Roman origin. When the Greeks built temples here *before* the Romans and called the city Heliopolis (city of the sun god), they were building on ruins that *already existed*! Baalbek was first mentioned in Assyrian writing under the name Ba'li as early as 804 BC. Like Tiahuanaco, the *real* Baalbek was a technical lay-out, a gigantic terrace composed of stone blocks, most of them with sides over 60 feet long and weighing up to 2,000 tons. This *platform* is incredibly old and has no historical date. The Greeks and Romans both made use of it. Even giving full rein to our imaginations, we cannot conceive that these stones were transported by the methods usually postulated by archaeologists. Wooden rollers? Sledges? Inclined planes? Sand tracks? What we can swallow with a little good-will in the case of Upper Egypt and other sites becomes sheer farce in the case of the stone blocks at Baalbek. These blocks could not have been moved with any of the known technical aids available in antiquity. Even today there is not a crane in the world powerful enough to lift a 2,000 ton block. My kingdom for a reasonable explanation of the method of transport! The ancient sanctuary of Baalbek dates back to the god of creation, Baal. Baal was glorified in the epic texts of Ugarit as 'Lord of the Heavens' or 'he who lords it on the mountain'. Baal was the same figure as Bel at Babylon, and Bel was identical with the gods Marduk and Enlil. Enlil was the 'god of the airs'. According to a cuneiform tablet, he spilt his seed into the womb of the earth maiden Meslamtaea. Mythology closes the circle.

143   The terrace at Baalbek in the Lebanon.

144   The 'Stone of the South', near Baalbek.

The remains of powerful, unknown civilisations lie on nearly all the inhabitable South Sea islands. Survivals of a very early, obviously highly developed technology disturb every visitor who has not come simply to take souvenir photos of these witnesses to the past. The stone 'documents' literally entice him to speculate and theorise.

Easter Island, discovered during Easter 1772, by the Dutchman Roggenveen, is the most easterly of the Polynesian islands in the Pacific Ocean. It belongs to Chile, has an area of 45 square miles and a present population of about 1,000. The island is of volcanic origin, has no trees, rises to a height of 1,845 feet and has two extinct volcanoes. Easter Island is a cornerstone in the mosaic of my 'world picture,' because of the hundreds of statues that are scattered round the island staring the visitor challengingly in the face. I know the theories of Thor Heyerdahl, whom I hold in high esteem. Nevertheless, after two lengthy visits to the island, I say that the hand-axe theory is not tenable in the face of the facts, which are 'hard' in the literal sense of the word. Finished, half-finished and just-begun statues lie about vertically and horizontally in the Rano Raraku crater. I have measured the distance from the untouched lava to individual statues and found spaces of up to six feet over a length of nearly 105 feet. Nobody could ever have freed the gigantic lumps of lava with small primitive stone tools. It is a fact that Heyerdahl found several hundred stone hand-axes at the foot of the crater. That seems to prove that someone worked with these tools at the work site. This is my theory. Alien cosmonauts supplied the original islanders with sophisticated technical tools that priests or magicians could use. They freed the masses from the lava and shaped them. Then the alien visitors disappeared. As usual the tools left behind were those which were blunt or unusable. I think it possible that the people who understood how to use them emigrated or died. The primitive people could not make new tools of the same calibre. It is a fact that the work stopped very suddenly. More than 200 unfinished statues 'cling' to the wall of the crater. Then the natives were seized with a wild ambition to complete the work.

As the 'old' tools were lacking, they attacked the lava with hand-axes. Day in, day out, the cheerful sound of hammering echoed from the crater wall all over the island, but their efforts were in vain. The stone tools got blunt and they were unable to detach a single statue from the rock face. Finally they gave up in disgust and left hundreds of hand-axes lying about in the crater. In opposition to Heyerdahl's theory, I consider the discovery of hand-axes as proof that the work could *not* have been carried out with *these tools*. And there is another important point that contradicts his theory. Let us take on trust the (unrealistic) possibility that the islanders did attack the lava in this way with hand-axes. When you plane a surface, shavings fall off. At some time or other even the best stonemason makes a mistake, splits an upper lip, scratches a nostril or cracks an eyelid. Yet the stonemasons of Easter Island must have worked faultlessly; every blow must have struck the right spot, for there is not a sign of error. Moreover, I have already mentioned the distances between the lava face and the statues. The debris from spaces measuring six by 105 feet cannot have disappeared into thin air, but there is none to be seen at Rano Raraku. The hand-axe theory may be acceptable for some of the smaller statues that were executed nearer to our own day. My conviction, shared by many visitors to Easter Island, is that it does not solve the puzzle of how the raw material was won from the volcanic stone. One has only to look at the mammoth figures, which are as much as 60 feet high and weigh 50 tons, to imagine how voluminous the mass of raw material must have been before the work began. If the Polynesians were the creators of the statues, no one has yet explained where they got the models for the shapes and expressions of the statues from. No member of any known Polynesian tribe has such characteristics: long, straight noses, tight-lipped mouths, sunken eyes and low foreheads. Nor can anyone say who is actually supposed to be depicted. Unfortunately, even Thor Heyerdahl does not know the answer to that.

I suspect that the same masters gave lessons on Easter Island, at Tiahuanaco, above Sacsayhuaman, in the Bay of Pisco and on the plain of Nazca, or at least that the same tools were used. Obviously it is only one of other possible theories and it could be rejected because of the vast distances between the various 'abodes' of my 'gods'. One premise for my interpretation is the acceptance of the fact that extraterrestrial beings did visit the earth. I assert that my theory has acquired a good deal more weight since I first introduced it. Now that my hypothesis that the prophet Ezekiel saw and described a spaceship has been proved, I cannot understand why people are not *also* prepared to admit that members of the spaceship's crew could have been active both as teachers and as donors of ultra-sophisticated tools. The know-alls may continue to doubt my theory, but at all events they must admit that it looks as if cutting the stone colossi out of the hard rock face was childs play to the original creators of the Easter Island statues. I am not impressed by the old arguments that alien cosmonauts could not have had the faintest interest in such activities. On the contrary, they had a vital interest in creating imperishable stone monuments, or having them created. I shall show why they were interested in a summary of my world picture.

147

150

148

151

149

152

153

154

147–154 These snapshots of Easter Island with its robot-like stone figures should help to prove my view that these sculptures could never have been made with primitive hand-axes. The statues were cut out of the rock enormous distances apart; height, 4 feet 3 inches, length, up to 15 feet (153–154). Intermediate spaces like this must have needed other tools than lightweight stone hand-axes.

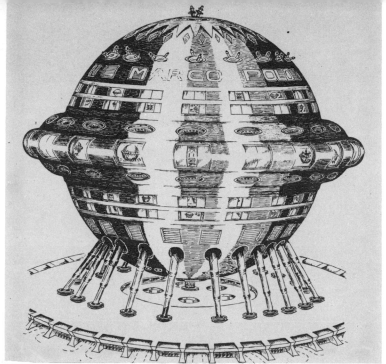

155

All spaceships built so far and even those in the planning stage are streamlined and pencil-shaped. They have to be like that, because with the rockets available today and their comparatively weak propulsion units, only objects which offer the most friction-free surfaces can pierce the 'wall' of the earth's atmosphere. But I am convinced that flying bodies of this shape are not ideal for interstellar traffic. Out there among the stars in airless space, a spaceship can have any conceivable shape so long as it is functional. NASA's Skylab, the first celestial laboratory, with its six extended solar-cell paddles (which are expected to produce 23 KW of electrical energy), looked as clumsy as a gigantic dustbin, with stilts and feelers leading in all directions. And the lunar module obviously no longer had to be built in the pencil shape. It was *box-like*, with four stilt-like legs, yet it shot into the orbit of the earth's satellite within seconds of receiving the command. In other words, where no atmosphere-like conditions have to be overcome, designs that reduce friction are unnecessary, indeed they can even be a nuisance because of their inevitable narrowness. Astronauts have to squeeze themselves through small hatches and narrow

156

tubes. In such cramped spaces, instruments and supply systems have to be arranged in tiers and all the apparatus for propelling the rocket has to be installed at the end, that is below.

A journey from star to star would be impossible with the liquid fuels available at present. The necessary fuel reserves, plus space for crew and apparatus, could not be transported into the universe. So spaceships for interstellar expeditions will not use rockets with liquid or solid fuel. Atomic units – perhaps nuclear fusion of hydrogen to helium –, units using photons or the reassembling of matter, will be available one day; for the time when technology will dispose of power as yet unimaginable is no longer in the unforeseeable future. One technical realisation in the form of quantums of electromagnetic radiation, called photons, will certainly be possible. They will reach a radiation speed approaching the speed of light and will be able to supply thrust for an almost unlimited period. In order to show how *un*-Utopian this idea is in comparison with current scientific discussions, I must tell you about Daniel Foreman, Technical Director of the Los Alamos Scientific Laboratory, New Mexico, which forms part of the University of California. Foreman works

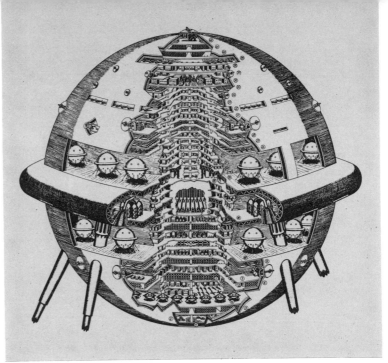

157

for the American Atomic Energy Commission and is especially
concerned with research on reactors for spaceflight. Foreman
says that at some time in the future the earth will burn out and
asks whether it could be taken to another galaxy before this
fatal hour arrives. 'The energy for this enormous undertaking,'
says Walter Sullivan, 'would be won from nuclear fusion, and
seawater could be used as the source of fuel.' But as the supply
of heavy water in the oceans would not be adequate, Foreman
suggested using reactions of the kind that take place in the
sun: the fusion of four hydrogen nuclei into one helium nucleus.
In his book *Signals from Space*, Sullivan wrote: 'Foreman
suggested using a quarter of this fuel for getting out of the sun's
gravitational field, keeping another quarter to steer the planet
into another solar system and retaining the remaining half for
locomotion between the stars, and light and heating on the
journey.' Foreman is convinced that this system of propulsion
for the earth could remain effective for eight milliard years and
'perhaps enable the planet to survive its own sun and reach solar
systems 1,300 light years away.' Please note that Foreman is

158

not a science-fiction writer; he conducted his dialogue with the plasma physics section of the American Physical Society. As I haven't got the necessary technical knowledge, the idea of transporting the whole world to another solar system would never have occurred to me! But serious scientists who are familiar with the future potentialities of technology are already talking about things that are even more incredible. Reverting once again to the problem of fuel for interstellar rockets, I should mention that the famous space biologist Carl Sagan, USA, says that it could be solved by in-flight fuelling with hydrogen which would supply the power for an interstellar jet propulsion unit. This type of gigantic spaceship would have to be assembled in a depot orbiting round the launching planet. Using the pickaback method, the parts of the giant construction would be shot into orbit and fitted together one after another. This would dispense with the necessity of the pencil shape from the beginning.

The problem remains that wherever the astronauts came from,

159

160

161

they would all be used to the gravity of their home world. But there is no gravity in a spaceship in outer space. On journeys lasting years or decades (time dilation!), the astronauts, who would be putting in a 'normal' working space-day, would need gravity. So gravity would have to be simulated. Did you ever swing a bucket of water round and round over your head at arm's length? Not a drop of water fell out, although the liquid was vertically above your head for the hundredth part of a second during the swinging. Owing to the swift rotation, the water stuck to the bottom of the bucket, or more accurately to the ceiling. The centrifugal force produced gravity; a field of gravity was simulated where none had existed before. There is no doubt that such artificial gravity could be produced in a spaceship, but the ship would have to be spherical in shape. Set in rotation, a simulated but genuinely effective gravity would be created at the outer edges, on the spaceship's equator. Then crews could be able to work without magnetic shoes; they could sleep lying down; they would not have to snatch their food

from the 'air', like birds. The floor of the crew's rooms would not lie in the direction of the propulsion unit, but horizontal to the line of flight. As we know, astronauts are buckled in during launching, backs to the propulsion unit. Once this is turned off and the spaceship is in 'free fall', it could be set in rotation around its own axis. Artificial gravity would be formed. It is logical that the work and recreation rooms would have to lie on the outer ring of the axis, for the familiar sensation of gravity would be most noticeable there. Spaceships with monstrous protuberances and projections are accident-prone: Skylab has given us dramatic proof of that. Antennae over a hundred yards long and solar energy sails with an area of 2,000 square yards that reach far out have a greater speed than the centre of the spaceship, when it is revolving on its own axis. They are put in great danger by a sudden change of course. Because of the artificial gravity that can be created the sphere is the ideal shape for friction-free interstellar flight, but in my view an oblate disc of the Flying Saucer type would also work.

159   Stylised illustration of a spherical spaceship on a ceremonial utensil (Anthropological Museum, Mexico).
160   Aztec ceremonial disc (serpentine). A theologically exaggerated depiction of an astronaut inside a sphere?
161   A several-thousand-year-old Dogu statuette, Japan, with unmistakable space traveller's features.
162   Groups of spheres on Moeraki Beach, New Zealand.

Spheres and discs can both be set in rotation. Interior decorators would install the room around the equator according to patterns established by industrial psychology. The whole surface of the spaceship's hull, even in rotation, could act as a solar cell for the transformation of energy. In space hardly any solar energy would be produced, but the amount expended would be very, very small, as the ship would be in free fall between the stars. Special machines, minireactors for example, would supply enough current for domestic purposes, though that would be the least of the designer's worries. What would a spherical spaceship look like? One of the most successful science-fiction series is called Perry Rhodan. For youthful readers spherical spaceships are an absolute must for space travel, as they are so used to their heroes shooting about the galaxy in spheres. The illustrators Rudolf Zengerle, Bernhard Stössel and Ingolf Thaler have used a lot of technical imagination in the drawings they have made of spherical spaceships in section. It is worthwhile looking closely at these imaginary drawings, for we should remember that technically-minded boys are becoming familiar with a phenomenon that they may yet experience in reality and which will come as no surprise to them. Surely nearly all science-fiction will soon be overtaken by sensational technical developments? To me myths, legends and early drawings and engravings seem to transmit memories of our technological future. Gods ride in 'flashing eggs' or 'land in heaven in pearls' or simply in spheres. In the National Anthropological Museum, Mexico, the leader of the gods is always depicted sitting in a sphere on so-called ceremonial wooden artefacts. Aztec ceremonial discs also show a sun god, working some kind of apparatus, inside a sphere. On cylinder seals, Sumerian gods emerge from spheres or ride on them. Egyptian deities from heaven wear spheres on their heads. There are spheres with tails of fire in the Valley of the Kings and winged spheres in the Temple at Luxor. The god Horus comes out of the 'world-egg'. The world-famous stele of Naram Sing, grandson of Sargon I, shows sun, moon and *next* to them a floating sphere at which warriors and musicians are gazing up. Are myths and plastic works of art based on confused memories of the past that give clues to what will be possible in the future?

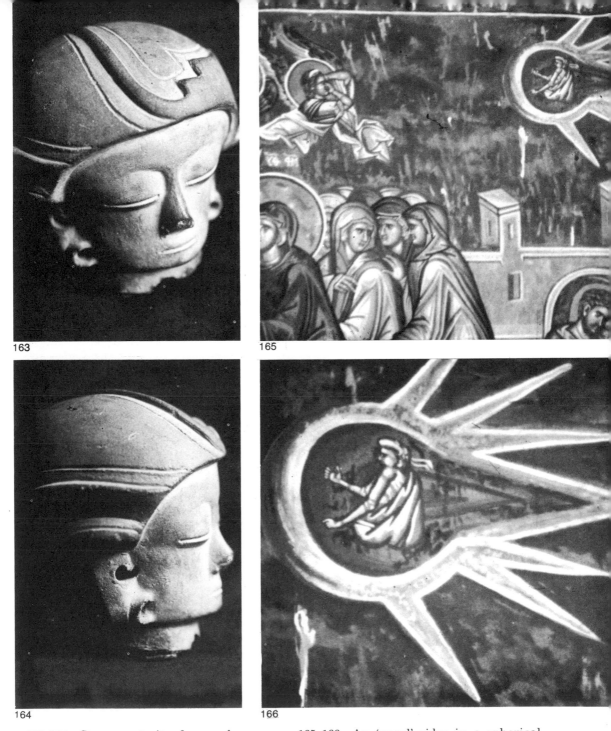

163   165

164   166

163–164 Stone portrait of an unknown race, a head with astronaut's helmet from the caves in Ecuador.

165–166 An 'angel' rides in a spherical flying object. From a mural in Desani Monastery, Jugoslavia.

167

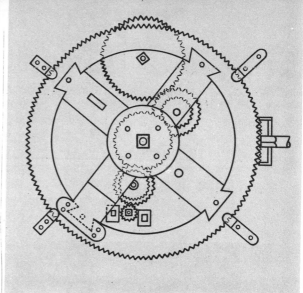

168

During Easter, 1900, a Greek sponge-diver's boat was driven on to the coast of the small southern island of Kythera by a storm. When the sea calmed down, Captain Kondos ordered his crew to dive for sponges again. They found the wreck of a ship at a depth of 180 feet and on board it strange blue vases, marble and bronze statues and unusual utensils. Salvage proved very difficult and in September 1901 diving operations were stopped. In the meantime it was ascertained that the ship had foundered in the first century BC. The archaeologist Valerios Stais came across a shapeless encrusted corroded lump while sorting out the material. When Stais examined this 'something' more closely, he found parts of a sophisticated mechanism with a very complex gear drive that must have worked like a differential gear. The whole machinery consists of about forty cog wheels, nine adjustable scales and three axes on a base plate. When the scales were deciphered, they only made the find more puzzling, for no instrument of this kind is mentioned or described in any classical text. The apparatus cannot be older than 100 BC. It is part of an astronomic calendar which showed the cycles and positions of the moon and the constellations. A calendar,

169

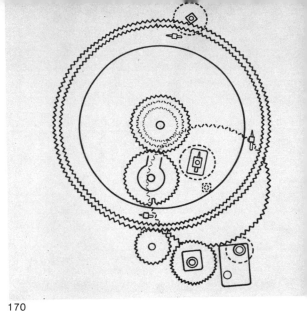

170

all right, but where did the machinery come from? Research
workers admit that there was no technology in the Hellenistic
age that could have produced this machine. Derek J. de Solla
Price says that the Greeks were not interested in experimental
science. Now every child knows that many experimental models
have to be made before a machine functions properly. That rule
applies equally to this case. The mystery begets new mysteries.
With what tools and instruments was the machinery made? For
they would have had to be developed first. The end product
must have been a sensational novelty in its day. Since it originated in a historical age, why is it never mentioned in contem-
porary texts, why has it neither forerunners nor descendants?
I have spoken to technicians and mathematicians who were
allowed to examine the machine from Antikythera in the
National Archaeological Museum at Athens. They all said its
accuracy was staggering, with errors of not more than 1/10 mm,
which was just as well, otherwise 40 cog wheels with a central
wheel with 240 teeth, each one 1·3 mm high, would soon have
given false values.
Who were the astronautical godparents who donated this
strange little present?

171

171 This petroglyph on a rock near Monte Alban, Mexico, undoubtedly portrays a technical apparatus. It is easy to make out a sharp drill, with handles and blades.

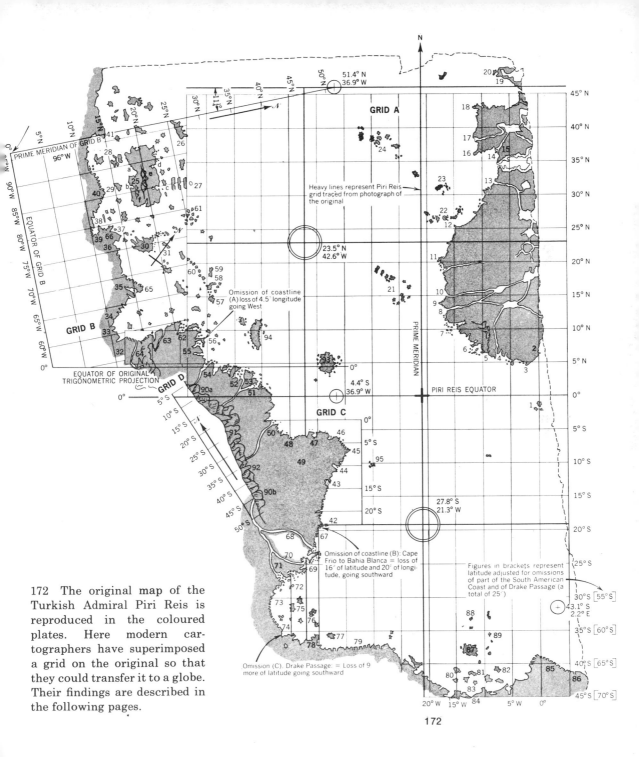

172 The original map of the Turkish Admiral Piri Reis is reproduced in the coloured plates. Here modern cartographers have superimposed a grid on the original so that they could transfer it to a globe. Their findings are described in the following pages.

GRID A

Heavy lines represent Piri Reis grid traced from photograph of the original

51.4° N
36.9° W

23.5° N
42.6° W

Omission of coastline (A) loss of 4.5° longitude going West

PRIME MERIDIAN OF GRID B
96° W

PRIME MERIDIAN

PIRI REIS EQUATOR

EQUATOR OF GRID B

GRID B

EQUATOR OF ORIGINAL TRIGONOMETRIC PROJECTION

GRID D

GRID C

4.4° S
36.9° W

27.8° S
21.3° W

Omission of coastline (B): Cape Frio to Bahia Blanca = loss of 16° of latitude and 20° of longitude, going southward

Figures in brackets represent latitude adjusted for omissions of part of the South American Coast and of Drake Passage (a total of 25°)

43.1° S
2.2° E

Omission (C). Drake Passage = Loss of 9 more of latitude going southward

173

174

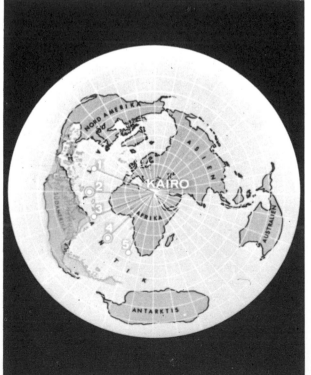

175

In 1929 the Topkapi Museum in Istanbul was turned into a Museum for Antiquities. On 9 November, B. Halil Edem, Director of the Turkish National Museum, found two fragments of a map by Piri Reis, who had held the office of Admiral of the Fleet in the Red Sea and the Persian Gulf. He began to draw the maps in the town of Gallipoli in 1513. In 1517, he gave them to the conqueror of Egypt, Sultan Selim I, while on a visit. Even before this find, Piri Reis was famous as a cartographer in Turkey, where they already possessed 215 maps drawn by him and commented on in his book *Bahriye*. These two pieces of a map drawn in delicate colours on gazelle hide were fragments of the Admiral's *Map of the World*, which had been believed lost. Piri Reis writes in *Bahriye*:

> They (the maps) were drawn by the wretched Piri Reis, son of Hadji Mehmet, who is known as brother son of Kemal Reis, in the town of Oelibolu (Gallipoli). God forgive them both in the month of the sainted Muharrem of the year 919 (9 March–7 April 1513).

In the 1940s copies of these fragments of a map of the world were acquired by several museums and libraries. In 1954 the sheets arrived on the desk of the American cartographer, Arlington H. Mallery, who had specialised in ancient charts for years. The sheets fascinated Mallery because they showed continents, the Antarctic for example, which had not been discovered in 1513.

Piri Reis says in *Bahriye* that he compiled his map of the world from twenty different maps and also that he used one of Christopher Columbus's maps for the coasts and islands of Antilia. (NB. None of Columbus's maps have yet been found.) Reis's notes contain details of America unknown to his contemporaries, but which he could have heard about from Columbus, who returned from his voyage of discovery in 1511. Theoretically that is possible, yet Piri Reis was convinced that his work was exceptional. He wrote: 'At this time no one possesses a map like this one.' Arlington Mallery asked his colleague Walters of the US Navy Hydrographic Institute to collaborate with him. Walters was immediately astounded by the accuracy of the distances between the Old and the New Worlds. At the beginning of the fifteenth century there was no map in existence showing America. The accurate placing of the

Canary Islands and the Azores was also astonishing. The two men noticed that Piri Reis had either not used the coordinates usual in his day or thought the earth was a disc. This puzzled them and in order to get to the bottom of the matter they made a grid with which they could transfer the old maps to a modern globe. Then their astonishment was complete. Not only the coastlines of North and South America, but also the outlines of the Antarctic fitted exactly where they belong according to our present state of knowledge. On Piri Reis's map of the world, the tip of South America sticks out from Tierra del Fuego in a narrow strip of land which then broadens out and joins up with Antarctica. *Today* stormy seas rage south of Tierra del Fuego. Piri Reis's map was compared millimetre by millimetre with outlines on the ocean bed prepared from the air by the most modern means, with the help of infrared photographs taken through the water and echo soundings from ships. It was established that about 11,000 years ago towards the end of the Ice Age this land bridge between South America and the Antarctic had actually existed! With painstaking accuracy Piri Reis had drawn in the coastlines, islands, bays and mountain peaks of the Antarctic. Today they can no longer be seen, because they are hidden under a covering of ice. During the International Geophysical Year in 1957, Father Lineham, then Director of Weston Observatory and Cartographer of the US Navy, examined the maps. He came to the same conclusion. The maps (especially the Antarctic areas) were incredibly accurate, with data which were not known to *us* until after the Swedish-British-Norwegian expeditions of 1949 and 1952. On 28 August 1958, Mallery and Lineham held a conference under the chairmanship of Mr Warren at the University of Georgetown. Here are some extracts from the records:

Warren: It is hard for us today to understand how cartographers could be so accurate so many centuries ago, seeing that we only discovered our modern scientific methods of mapmaking quite recently.

Mallery: That was obviously a problem we puzzled over . . . At any rate we can't imagine how they could have made such accurate maps without the help of aircraft. The fact remains that they did and what is more, they fixed the degrees of longitude absolutely correctly, something we couldn't do until two hundred years ago.

Warren: Father Lineham, you took part in the seismic research of the Antarctic. Do you share the enthusiasm over these new discoveries?

Lineham: I certainly do. Using the seismic method we found out things which seemed to support a lot of the drawings on the maps: the land masses, the projection of the mountains, the seas, the islands . . . I think that with the seismic method we can 'remove' still more ice from the countries that are drawn on the maps and that will show that they are even more accurate than we are inclined to believe at present . . .

In the meantime, the grand old man of cartography, Professor Charles Hapgood, studied Piri Reis. During correspondence with the US Air Force, which had mapped the Antarctic, Hapgood received this letter from Commander Harold Z. Ohlmeyer on 6 July, 1960: 'The coastlines must have been mapped before the Antarctic was covered with ice. Today the ice in this region is about a mile thick. We have no idea how the data on this map could have been compiled with the geographical knowledge available in 1513.'

The Piri Reis maps are tangible evidence in support of my theory that we had visitors from the cosmos in the past. To me it is obvious that extraterrestrial spacemen made the maps from space stations in orbit. During one of their visits they made our ancestors a present of the maps. They survived for millennia as holy objects and finally came into the admiral's hands. When he drew his map of the world, he did not realise what he was depicting. When the Piri Reis maps are compared with modern ones, the errors are minimal:

Present geographical position	Piri Reis	Errors compared with today
Gibraltar		
36°N 5° 5'W	35°N 7°W	1°S 1° 50'W
The Canary Islands		
27°–29°N 13°–17°W	26°–28°N 14°–20°W	1°S 1°W
Gulf of Venezuela		
11°–12°N 71°W	10°–11°N 65°W +4° 50'	0°S –1° 50'E

176–180 Sete Cidades, in the State of Piaui, Brazil, the 'Seven Cities' about which scholars have puzzled without finding an answer. Artificial constructions, freakish natural formations, or a combination of both?

176

177

178

179

180

How many people have the leisure to think about all the unsolved puzzles there are in our little world? How many people
have the opportunity of seeing them? I have made it my job to
seek out these mystery-enshrouded places and introduce my
readers to them. At the invitation of the authorities of Piaui,
Brazil, I visited Sete Cidades (Seven Cities), which lie north of
Teresina between the little town of Piripiri and the Rio Longe.
It is not really certain whether they consist of ruins destroyed
by great heat or rock eroded by nature, but *I* sense a plan
behind all the disorder. There are seven districts which seem to
have been connected by roads. There are no 'ruins', no monoliths, no stones in layers, no steps or staircases, no material
that has obviously been worked by the hand of man. It is a
mysterious place. If the rocks of Sete Cidades were eroded, why
not the surrounding rocks too? Where do the crumbling masses
of metal that drip from the walls like red tears come from? I am
familiar with the usual bands of minerals that form bizarrely
shaped geological strata in stone. Here these bands run dead
straight and horizontal, then suddenly turn at right angles to
continue upwards or downwards in a straight line. There are
blisters as big as one's thumb as if the rock had 'cooked' at
some time in the past. What happened here? The rock paintings
are established facts. You can see, touch and photograph them.
They are much more recent than the stones in their vicinity.
Once again we do not know who made the drawings in this
apocalyptic landscape, or when, but we are familiar with the
subjects from several other sites. Sete Cidades has two 'doubles':
'Sete Cidades' in the Atlantic (Canary Islands) and 'Sete Cidades'
in Australia, in Arnhem Land, south-east of Darwin.
The legends of the three 'Seven Cities' seem to be related. I
shall have more to say about them.

181

The Caroline Islands form the largest archipelago in Micronesia in north-west Oceania, with a total area of 617 square miles. The largest of the 1,500-odd islands, with an area of 183 square miles, is Ponape, which is surrounded by many islets. One of them, about the size of the Vatican City, is officially called Temuen, but is known as Nan Madol because of the massive ruins of that name. Once again the period when the vast complex was built has not been dated, nor do we know who the constructors were. The only historical fact is that when the Portuguese navigator Pedro Fernandes de Quiros landed in Temuen from the *San Geronimo* in 1595, the buildings were already shown to the white men as ruins. As we do not know the origin of the buildings, we are groping in the dark when we ask what they mean or what purpose they served. Why did someone at some point in time take the colossal trouble to move some 400,000 basalt blocks from the north coast of Ponape where the basalt was quarried, to this remote islet? If 'temples' had to be built, why weren't they erected near the quarries? Even today the walls of the ruins are more than 125 feet high in places and up to 2,580 feet long. If assembling the 12- to 27-foot blocks, often weighing more than 10 tons, must have been laborious, their transport through the trackless virgin forest, even by an army of strong men, is quite incredible. If, working round the clock, four basalt blocks weighing several tons were quarried, dressed and taken to Nan Madol from the north coast every day, it would have taken 296 years to complete this crazy task. In all ages there was only room for a very few men on the tiny island. So where did the vast but necessary host of workmen come from? Nan Madol is not a 'beautiful' city; its architecture is sober and utilitarian, with none of the exuberant display of other South Sea edifices. It was certainly a fortress. In his book *Der masslose Ozean* Herbert Rittlinger says Ponape was once the centre of a splendid kingdom and that pearl divers had scoured the seabed for treasure and told stories of columns and coffins. Under the Japanese, platinum became *de facto* the main export, yet there is no platinum in the local island stone.

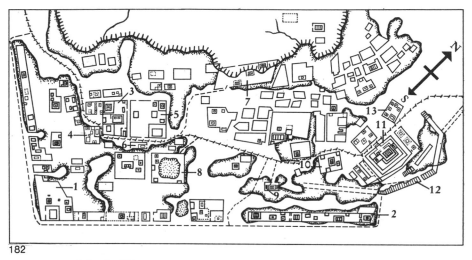

Island of Temuen
Symbols:

☐ House foundations	------------- Incomplete buildings
☐ Foundations with hearths	-------- Canal
▨ Burial vaults	~~~~~~~~~~ Main canal

Through the clear water I could see buildings in the sea which
linked up with the island and were continued there by buildings
in a similar style of architecture, which led to the 'sacred well'.
Supposing it was not a well but the entrance to an underground
lay-out? Were the buildings meant to protect the entrance?
South Sea islanders would not have been able to construct such
underground structures. Did strange visitors help them in this?
Legend tells of a flying fire-breathing dragon which excavated
the canals and so created the islets, and about his magician
helper, who used a magic spell to make the basalt blocks fly
across. Help by alien astronauts does not satisfy me as an
explanation, either. Why did they seek out this miserable little
islet? But this objection also applies to the South Sea islanders,
if they were in fact the builders. What we are left with is one of
the many unsolved puzzles on our ancient planet.

183

184

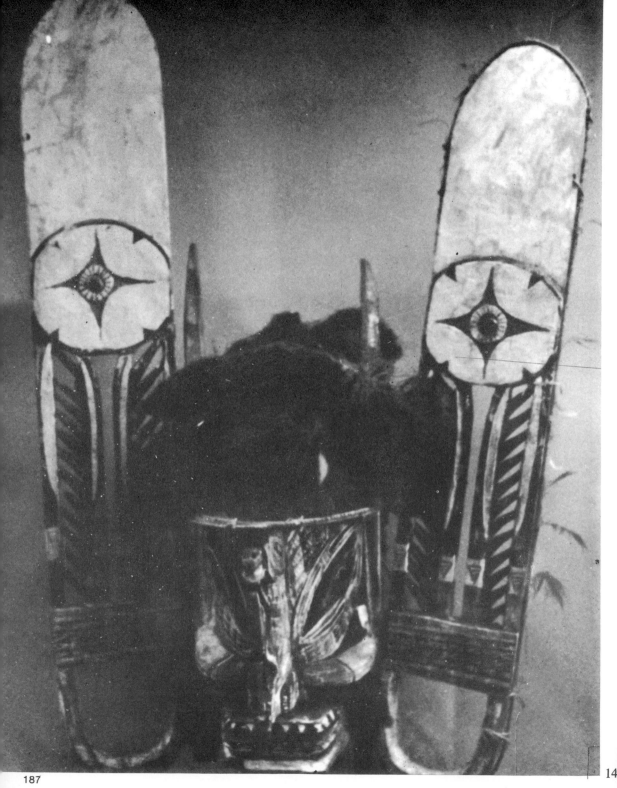

The South Sea islands between Australia, Indonesia and the islands near the coast of South America in the Pacific Ocean have a surface area of 480,000 square miles and occupy an area of sea covering 21 million square miles. On them live the Papuans, Melanesians, Polynesians and Micronesians. Treasures from the islanders' history are preserved in many museums. For example, ritual masks of the South Sea islanders are on show in Auckland, New Zealand, and in the Bishop Museum, Honolulu.

They pulled these masks over their faces and tried to imitate the movements of flight in ritual dances. Today I think it is easy to recognise poor copies of one-man flying machines in these so-called ritual masks. Pulled over the head, the flat side-pieces which could be moved downwards were imitations of wings. One can see the holes at the lower end for putting one's arms through. Even the arm and leg supports, and the corset into which the aviator had to squeeze himself have remained in the memory of Polynesian folk artists for thousands of years. Obviously the islanders no longer know *why* they adorn their gods, kings and chieftains with such complicated apparatuses. No one can *fly* with such gear, yet the flying wardrobe of the strange visitors became part of the islanders' folklore. Ritual masks? Excuse my mirth!

187 Ritual mask from the Auckland Museum, New Zealand.

188 According to the Maori legend, the God Pourangahua flew from his legendary dwelling Hawaike to New Zealand, seated on a magic bird.

188

189

189   The Salesian Father Carlo Crespi in the patio of the Church of
Maria Auxiliadora at Cuenca.

Father Carlo Crespi, who comes from Milan, has lived in the small town of Cuenca, Ecuador, for more than 50 years. He is a priest of the Church of Maria Auxiliadora. Crespi was accepted by the Indians as a real friend. They used to bring him presents from their hiding places. Finally the father had so many precious objects stored in his house and the church that one day he received permission from the Vatican to open a museum. This museum in the Salesian School at Cuenca grew and grew until in 1960 it was one of the biggest museums in Ecuador, and Crespi was recognised as an archaeological authority. But he has always been a rather embarrassing servant of his church, for he asserts vehemently that he can prove that there was a direct connection between the Old World (Babylon) and the New World (pre-Inca civilisations); and that goes right against prevailing opinion. On 20th July 1962 there was an act of arson and the father's museum was burnt down. What Father Crespi managed to salvage is housed today in two long narrow rooms, which are in a terrible muddle. Brass, copper, sheet-metal, zinc, tin and wooden objects and in the midst of them all pure gold, sheet-gold, silver and sheet-silver. Nowadays hurried visitors claim that the old man, who is ninety now, is senile and incapable of telling brass from gold. They say he owns nothing but worthless junk made by present-day Indians and palmed off on him. It is true that Crespi is no longer in possession of all his mental powers, but he was when he built his museum as a renowned archaeologists during the best years of his life. It was no junk yard. All the objects I show here come from the famous Crespi Museum. They were saved from it and are not modern forgeries. Most of the pieces came from the underground hiding places of which the Indians know so many. All the motifs date to Inca or pre-Inca times; there are no Christian symbols among them. In Crespi's collection there are metal and stone sculptures of completely unknown animals, antediluvian monsters, figures from myths and legends, many-headed snakes and birds with six legs. Elephants appear on gold and silver plaques. Elephant bones *have* been found in North America and Mexico and dated to 12,000 BC. There were no elephants left in South America in the age of the Incas, whose civilisation, it has been established, began around 1200 BC. Either the Incas were visited by elephants from Africa or the pictures are more than 12,000 years old. Either . . . or.

190

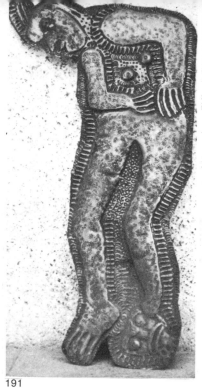

191

192

193

194

195

196

197

190–197 Eight figurative pieces from Crespi's collection. Each piece hides a mystery. So far none of them has been explained. Looked at with an open mind, each one contains emblems that are universally relevant.

198–202 This metal plaque probably tells a continuing story. The individual vertical sections show, in bewildering profusion, detailed compositions that merge with one another. Crespi, a highly respected archaeologist in the best years of his life, is convinced that this 'cartoon' dates to pre-Inca times. To stimulate the reader's imagination the sections outlined in white on the panel have been enlarged. A face with a solar crown and undeciphered signs (199); a giraffe-like head with rays, between which the delicate treatment of the metal is visible (200); a monkey-like head from which eyes grow like polyps (201) and an obviously deliberate connection of three heads with rays protruding (202). The whole thing is a fascinating problem-picture.

199

200

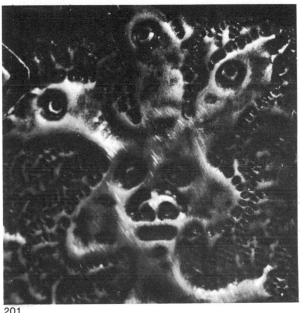

201

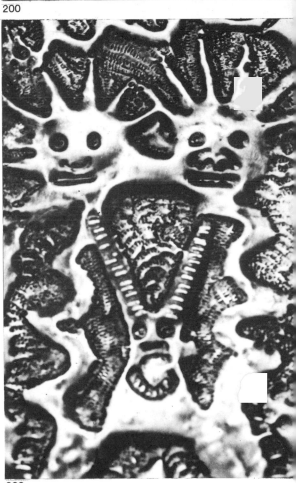

202

203

204

206

207

203 A stone tablet with
transitions from ideograms
to writing.
204 Stone tablet with 25
Indian characters.
205 Stone pyramid. Above
the characters is an
elephant.
206 Gold sheet with a picture of an Egyptian pyramid
unknown in South America.
The letters at the foot of the
pyramid enlarged (207).

154

205

Are the characters on the metal reliefs at Cuenca older than all known writing? Cuneiform writing in Phoenicia and hieroglyphs in Egypt are supposed to have originated around 2000 BC from a mixture of Egyptian and Babylonian influences. The pre-Israelite population of Palestine is supposed to have created a simplified syllabic script with 100 signs, composed of a mixture of both the foregoing kinds of writing. The Phoenician alphabet developed from this about 1700 BC. Scholars claim that the Incas had no script in the alphabetical sense of the word. They did have quipus, a language of knots, but it had no connection with written characters. What do the ethnologists and South American experts say about the characters from Cuenca? 56 different letters or symbols exist. I should like to know what message they contain. Compared with this burning question I consider an analysis of the metal alloys on which they are engraved to be of secondary importance.

208

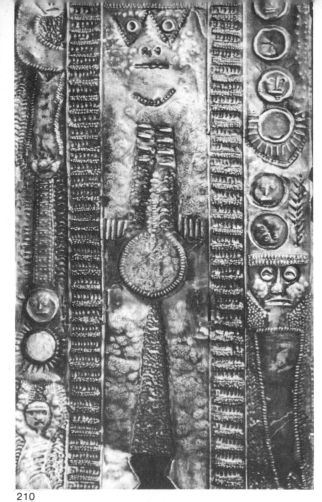

210

209

211

212

213

214

215

208–215   The supreme ruler of the Incas and presumably of the pre-Inca tribe, too, was the 'Son of the Sun'. Possibly this descendant of the sun was portrayed here, for the sun shines on top of the head-band (208, 209). To left and right run films whose frames show events in the solar system, in my opinion.

The sculpture (210) also exhibits ideograms with representations of the sun. In the lower left corner (211) a child is born from the sun. Pre-Inca works constantly provide visual evidence of my theory that snakes had their appropriate place in mythological accounts (212–215).

216

216–225 Even today the mythological images on this silver-zinc disc are most mysterious and quite inexplicable. They must be more than mere artistic flourishes. The enlargements may encourage the reader to form his own ideas.

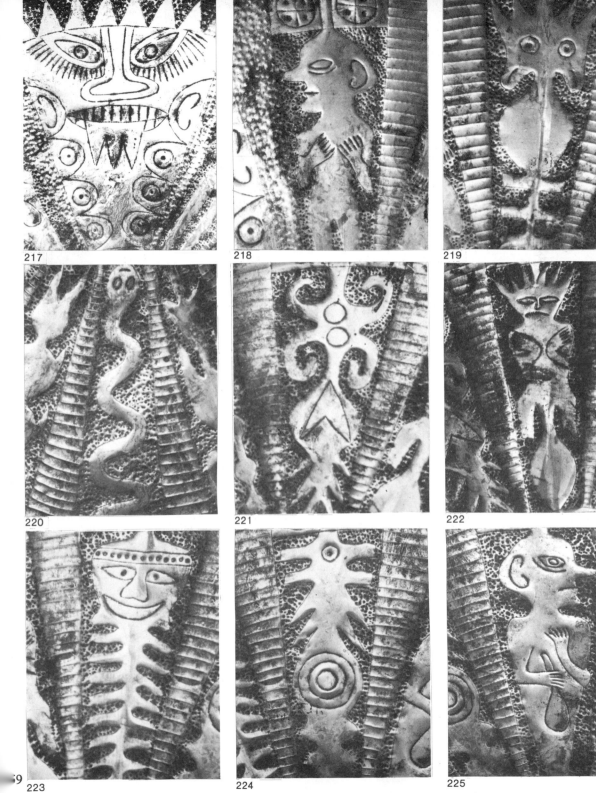

217

218

219

220

221

222

223

224

225

226

227

226–229 In a shed belonging to the church Father Crespi keeps 30 engraved silver sheets from 30 to 78 feet long and with an average width of 4 feet 2 inches. Forgeries! say the know-alls. What originals are supposed to have been forged? And if an Indian 'forger' really invented all the motifs from his own head, he must have been a genius and a philanthropist into the bargain. Who voluntarily hammers and engraves sheets over 60 feet long (and for whom)? To make a present of them to the Father? In addition this fabulous 'forger' must have been a very rich man, for the raw material is by no means cheap.

228   229

227–228   Two of many sheet-gold steles. The sun shines down on a paradisal idyll.

When Pioneer F (Jupiter F) was shot into the heavens in March 1972, it was the first satellite due to leave our solar system. In April 1973, the ship passed through the dangerous asteroid belt without damage and is now rushing past Jupiter into outer space. As the theoretical possibility exists that Pioneer F may be under way for thousands of years, it could even be located and captured by alien intelligences. To provide the ship with a passport – who? when? whence? – for this eventuality, the American astrophysicists and exobiologists Carl Sagan and Frank Drake inscribed a coded message on a gold-covered aluminium plaque. It contained information for unknown recipients. Sagan and Drake started from the premise that any alien intelligence would be familiar with a hydrogen atom, and that they would also know the binary system of numerals, for it is the language of all logically built computers and should be most easily understood. On it is engraved the schematic outline of the flight-path the ship will follow from earth to Jupiter; above stand a man and a woman; behind them the sun and at their feet our solar system. Provided alien intelligences know the binary system of numbers, they could decipher all the data. But what would happen if such a ship had suddenly landed in the midst of the Inca civilisation? They knew nothing about binary numbers, nothing about the structure of the hydrogen atom. The finders would have taken the gold plaque (poor Crespi, it was only aluminium covered with gold!) to their ruler and he would have handed it on to the son of the sun, the king. No-one would have been able to interpret the drawings and symbols, but they would have ordered an accurate account of how and when this message from the gods landed on earth. A thing that fell from the heavens must have come from the gods! The exalted authorities would have given orders for copies to be made and placed in the temples in honour of the gods. I wonder whether similar messages have not hit our planet long ago. Are they lying in temples and museums at this very moment? Are they in the earth, just waiting to be found? 'Discoveries' like the plaque from Cuenca on the opposite page make me ask what this skeleton with 44 dots round its skull is meant to express. The skeleton stands on a zigzag line and ten dots. On the right hand border the symmetry is suddenly dropped. Ten diagonal lines each have a varying number of

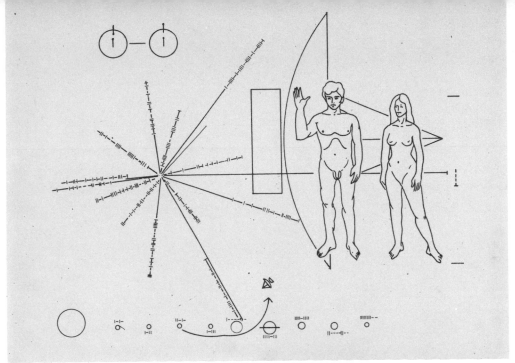

230

231

232 Anyone who has stood in front of the treasures – and the rubbish – in Crespi's church and been allowed to rummage in it, finds it very hard to give even an approximate idea of all the unexplained material. I have tried to do so in the preceding illustrations, which are amplified later in the magnificent section of coloured plates. When the white conquerors invaded South America, all non-Christian symbols were destroyed, wiped out. Under the barbaric dominion of the Inquisition no Inca artist dared use traditional symbols and images. As none of the pictures shown here contains Christian ornaments, I should like to say that I agree with Father Crespi, now a little senile, who said in his best years: 'All these representations date to the pre-Inca period'.

dashes on them. People would have thought about them if they had been on the Pioneer plaque, why not think about these too?

> Viracocha, Lord of the world!
> Thou art neither man, nor woman,
> Lord of adoration.
> Thou art he works magic
> Even with spittle.
> Who are thou?
> Show thyself to thy son!
> Whether he be below, or above
> or perhaps out there in the universe . . .

So says a prayer to Viracocha handed down by the chroniclers. Viracocha was Inca's supreme deity, he was looked on as the highest and ultimate creator and begetter of all other gods; he was simultaneously man and woman. It is assumed that he was worshipped at Tiahuanaco. But Viracocha was also the teacher of his people, who owed their knowledge to him. After the creation was finished and he had left instructions behind, he disappeared into the sky, but not before he had promised to return one day. Probably Viracocha fulfilled the same function for the Incas as Kukulkan did for the Mayas and Quetzalcoatl for the Aztecs.

The Brazilian linguistic scholar, Lubomir Zaphyrov, who specialises in Inca studies, has established that some 120 compound Inca words are still used today by the Chuwashen, a Tartaro-Finnish people in Russia. They are precisely explained by about 170 simple Chuwashen words. Zaphyrov says that most of the words that have been preserved come from Inca mythology. Here are a few examples:

Viracocha = The good spirit from space

Kon Tkis Illa Viracocha = Ruler of highest origin, radiant like lightning, the good spirit from space

Chuvash = God out of the light

There are still a lot of nuts for comparative philologists to crack!

233

234

234–237 This 4½-inch-high gold pectoral of the Mixtec God of the Dead Mictlantecutli is housed in the Regional Museum at Oaxaca (Mexico). The pectoral was found in a tomb near Monte Alban. What does the ornamentation on the god's chest mean? Was it simply a whim of the artist? Or was a primordial technical model available? In fact, it is quite easy to deduce a modern electronic integrated circuit from the chest decoration!

238 A pre-Inca vase from the underground caves at Cuenca, Ecuador.

239 Gold model aircraft. Gold Museum, Bogota, Colombia.

235

236

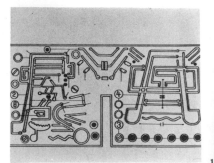

237

238

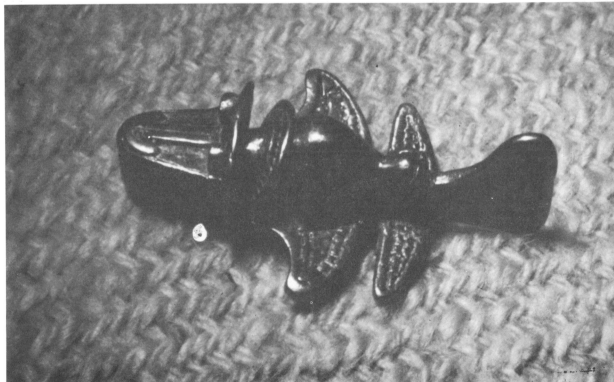

239

240

241

Contact was first made with the Kayapo Indians living on the upper reaches of the Amazon in Brazil in 1952. The strange straw garments worn by the Kayapos at all their festivities are important evidence for my theories. Joao Americo Peret, one of the outstanding Indian scholars, narrated the Kayapos' creation myth to me. According to this legend an unknown number of generations ago an earthquake with smoke and fire took place on a nearby mountain. The inhabitants fled to their village in terror. After a few days some young warriors plucked up courage and tried to kill the stranger who emerged from the earthquake, but poisoned arrows, lances and clubs bounced off him and he laughed the bold warriors to scorn. But the stranger stayed with our ancestors in the village. The inhabitants got used to his presence and learnt the language of the Kayapos from him. He also taught them many tricks for using weapons when hunting, he set up the first school, the young men's house, and taught them the laws of agriculture. The stranger was called Bep Kororoti, which means 'I come from space'. One day, the legend still relates today, Bep Kororoti put on his strange gleaming white suit again and told them that his time was up. He would be 'fetched' and no one must follow him. Nevertheless some curious youngsters sneaked after him when he went up the mountain. They saw smoke and fire again and heard a terrible noise . . . and they saw the stranger disappearing heavenwards. In memory of this heavenly teacher, says Peret, the Kayapo Indians still wear the strange straw suits which are pale copies of the god's spacesuit.

I should make it quite clear that the photos opposite were taken in 1952 – long before Gagarin (1961) made the first space-flight. So the spacesuit was not yet known as the fashionable gear for all astronauts, and the Kayapos on the Upper Amazon, who cannot read the printed word, let alone reports of space flights, still do not know what is worn in space today. But this straw spacesuit, an important requisite of the past, is as old as the traditional myth.

Do the Kayapo Indians preserve in this way very early memories which we are seeking to recapture today – but not nearly hard enough?

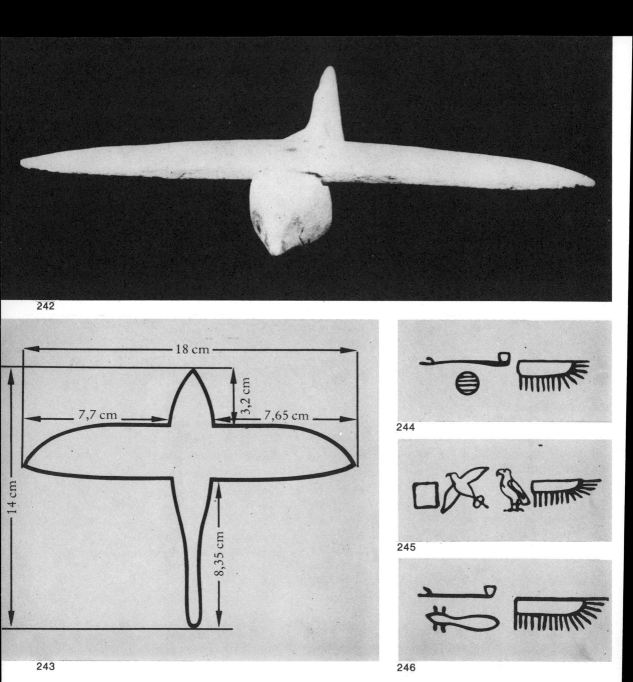

242

243

244

245

246

244–246 These are the three Ancient Egyptian hieroglyphs which express the wish: 'I want to fly'.

The desire to be able to fly is as old as mankind. Whole philosophies grew up round this wish. The first reference to it is recorded in an Ancient Egyptian hieroglyphic inscription. There are three hieroglyphs which mean: 'I want to fly'. Egyptologists cannot find much to say about this translation, which is their own work. In 1898 a model was found in a tomb near Sakkara. It was labelled 'Bird' and catalogued as such in the Egyptian museum at Cairo. It stayed there for fifty years, numbered 6347 among a host of other Ancient Egyptian 'birds'. Not until 1969 was this strange bird kicked out of the nest. A cuckoo's egg was hatched. Dr Khalil Messiha was startled when he saw the bird. Unlike all the other birds, No 6347 not only had straight wings, but also a high upright tailfin. Dr Messiha examined the strange bird and found a sign engraved on it saying 'Pa Diemen' which means 'Gift of Amon' in Ancient Egyptian. Who was Amon? Amon was 'Lord of the airbreath', underwent symbiosis with the sun god Ra and was elevated to 'God of Light'. Today it is accepted without question that No 6347 is a model aircraft. It is made of wood, weighs 39·12 grammes and is in good condition. The wingspan is 18 cm, the aircraft's nose is 3·2 cm long and the overall length is 14 cm. The extremities of the aircraft and the wingtips are aerodynamically shaped. Apart from a symbolic eye and two short lines under the wings, it has no decorations nor has it any landing legs. Experts have tested the model and pronounced it airworthy. They say it has ideal proportions. After this sensational discovery, the Minister for Culture, Mohammed Gamal El Din Moukhtar, commissioned a technical research group to put other birds under the microscope. The team nominated on 23 December 1971 consisted of Dr Henry Riad, Director of the Museum of Egyptian Antiquity, Dr Abdul Quader Selim, Deputy Director of the Egyptian Museum for Archaeological Research, Dr Hismat Nessiha, Director of the Department of Antiquities, and Kamal Naguib, President of the Egyptian Aviation Union. On 12 January 1972, the first exhibition of Ancient Egyptian model aircraft was opened in the Hall of the Egyptian Museum for Antiquities. Dr Abdul Quader Hatem, Representative of the Prime Minister, and the Air Minister Ahmed Moh presented fourteen Ancient Egyptian model aircraft to the public.

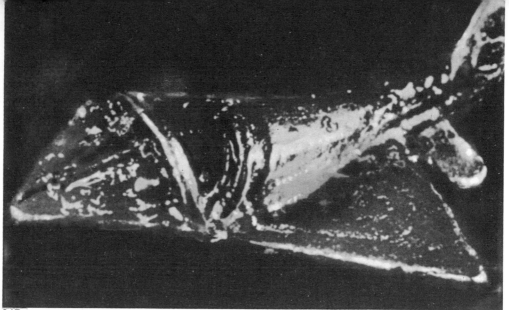

247

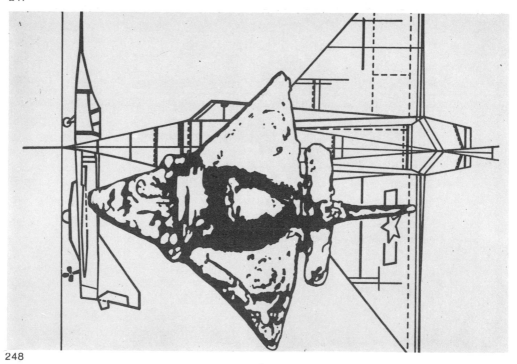

248

247–248 This gold model aircraft is on show in the State Museum, Bogota. Archaeologists catalogued it as a 'religious ornament', until the Aeronautical Institute, New York, examined the model. Technical tests proved its airworthiness.

1

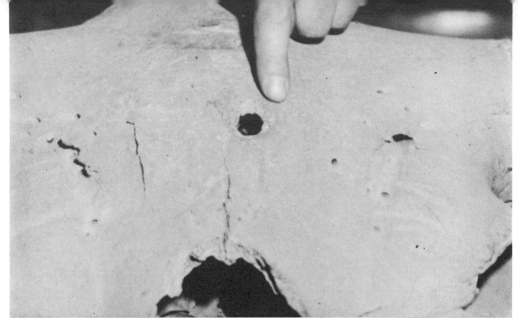

249

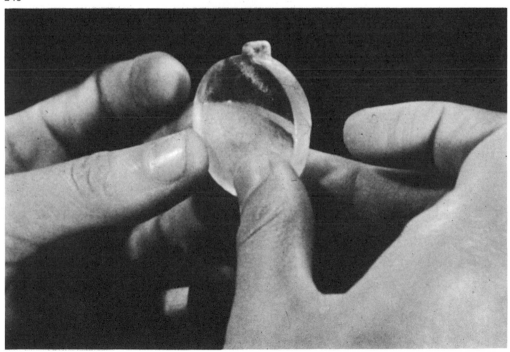

250

249 This section of a bison's skull is preserved in the Anthropological Museum, Moscow. You can clearly see the hole made by a bullet entering. This find is 10,000 years old. Who had modern weapons in those days?

250 This crystal lens from a tomb in Helwan, Egypt, is now in the British Museum. It was mechanically ground and surprisingly enough no one disputes this!

251

252

251 This ceramic object was found on a terrace of the Great Pyramid at Tlateloco, at a depth of 18 feet. Today it is in the Anthropological Museum, Mexico. Officially described as an 'incense-burner', the whole thing looks like a bad copy of a jet engine.

252 Yet another curiosity! This galvanic battery, from which one can still coax 1·5 volts, is in a showcase in the Iraq Museum, Baghdad.

253

254

Archaeologists' spades daily turn up curiosities that can only be fitted into the existing system of classification with great difficulty. But they manage it. Otherwise what could they say about a stone amulet found in Ecuador that a Stone Age man wore round his neck? The manikin is standing on a sphere, and that is remarkable because no Stone Age man knew that we live on a sphere. Model aircraft of various dimensions are found both in Father Crespi's collection and the Gold Museum at Bogota. Most of them are cast in heavy gold. What models were used to make them? If Ezekiel could describe a spaceship in all its detail in the year 592 BC, why shouldn't pre-Inca tribes have seen and modelled an aeroplane? Surely it is acceptable to credit the cosmonauts with aircraft for use over shortish distances? Why not? People who could build spaceships, would also have aircraft of all sizes. Pre-Inca tribes saw them, copied them and put them in the tombs of their rulers as divine gifts.

255

256

255 The look-out holes in the circular building of the Mayan Observatory at Chichen Itza are not directed at the brightest stars, as would be logical, but at the stars of the Mayan mythology, which tells of an origin from outer space.

256 The calendar pyramid also stands at Chichen Itza. Each step corresponds to a day, each platform to a Maya month. When 365 steps had been built, the temple was erected on the top.

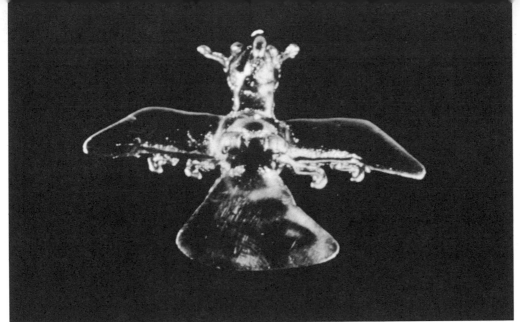

257

258

257–258 Two gold models of aeroplanes
from a private collection in Colombia.

259

The clay plate illustrated above dates to the Toltec period
(Mexico). It is a perfect example of how one can look at an object
from two points of view. From the archaeological point of view
it is a 'decorated clay plate'. I ask the reader to adopt my stand-
point for once. Cover up the inner circle with the Indian's face.
What is left in the outer circle gives the impression of an electric
apparatus. All the operating details are recognisable: the copper
coils, the carbons, the entrances and exits of the leads, etc. The
likeness of the Indian might represent the man who invented the
machine or was working it. The right-hand page shows the
facsimile of a Sanskrit manuscript. The International Academy
of Sanskrit Research at Mysore, India, was the first body to
venture to translate a Sanskrit text by Maharashi Bharadwaja,
a seer in the remote past, into terms intelligible to our modern
world. The result was staggering. Old concepts turned into
aeroplanes with their alloys and weapons. The text tells of the
secret of making planes invisible, of the uncanny possibility
of hearing conversations inside enemy planes and taking them
down. All honour to the brave men of Mysore.

THE INTERNATIONAL ACADEMY OF SANSKRIT RESEARCH,

MYSORE, INDIA

महर्षि भरद्वाजप्रणीत

वैमानिक शास्त्रम्

/ A MANUSCRIPT FROM THE PRE HISTORIC PAST /

AERONAUTICS

BY

Maharshi Bharadwaja

Some Sample Extracts:

अथारभ्यायमानायुगे मणिपूरे महाहरम् ।

प्रगमामिसंस्कारकरण शुभम् नृणाम् ॥

अनयासाद्गमयानस्थ्यूष्टानसाधकम् ।

सानर्थि मानवेधिव्यसनास्रकषायकम् ॥

वैमानिकविद्यार्थ व्यक्ते ऽस्मिन् बहुविधि ॥

पृथिव्याम्नन्तरिक्षे च जलच्छेगमखस्ववम् ।

यस्समर्थो जवेनासु स विमान इति स्मृतः ॥

देशाद्देशान्तरं महद्वीपाद्द्वीपान्तरं तथा ।

लोकाल्लोकान्तरं वापि वोऽऽम्बरे गमुमर्हति ।

स विमान इति प्रोक्तो देशयानविदां वरैः ॥

अनेदच्छाच्छेद्यमग्नायुग्भावविनाशनादिगुण्रविशिष्टं

विमानरचनाक्रियारहस्यम् ।

विमानस्तम्भनरहस्यम्

विमानाद्दृश्यकरणरहस्यम्

परविमानस्थ प्रसंगश्रवणादि सम्वादाकर्णनरहस्यम्

परविमानस्थरूपाकर्षणरहस्यम्

परयानागमनसंकेतप्रज्ञनरहस्यम्

"In this book are described in 9 pregnant and captivating chapters, the art of manufacturing various types of Aeroplanes of smooth and comfortable travel in the sky, as a unifying force for the Universe, contributive to the well being of mankind."

"That which can go by its own force, like a bird, on earth, or water, or in air, is called 'Vimaana'."

"That which can travel in the sky, from place to place, land to land, or globe to globe, is called 'Vimaana' by scientists in Aeronautics."

"The secret of constructing aeroplanes, which will not break, which cannot be cut, will not catch fire, and cannot be destroyed.

The secret of making planes motionless

The secret of making planes invisible

The secret of hearing conversations and other sounds in enemy planes

The secret of receiving photographs of the interior of enemy planes

The secret of ascertaining the direction of enemy planes' approach

260

261

261 The author taking measurements at Sacsayhuaman.

Australia, the smallest continent, with an area of about three million square miles and only 11·5 million inhabitants, is becoming increasingly interesting to prehistorians. Since young Australian scholars have begun to explore the vast terrain in helicopters and Land Rovers, all kinds of reports have come in which prove the continent without a history had an extremely fascinating past. The two young Leyland brothers from New Castle have made wonderful coloured documentary films of aboriginal rock and cave paintings in central Australia, near Alice Springs. Once again we find the 'international symbols' such as circles, squares, suns, wavy lines and *naturally* (I say!) figures in astronauts' suits with helmets. A monolith engraved with a figure in a bulky suit and large helmet was found in Arnhem Land, west of Darwin. He could be a twin brother of the great Martian god in the Sahara! From Laura, Queensland, comes the image of a man flying, as if he were not subject to gravity. Drawings of godlike figures with gigantic antennae on their heads were found about six miles east of Alice Springs, on the rocks of the Ndahla gorge. There, too, Robert Edwards discovered faces of gods wearing protective goggles, engraved on the rock. Lines that cross each other or run parallel to each other only to end abruptly, are engraved on a rock 4 feet 7 inches long and 3 feet wide. I automatically thought of the network of lines on the plain of Nazca, Peru. A plaster-of-paris copy is in the museum at Adelaide. Rock drawings with the subjects now familiar to us were tracked down in Yarbiri Soak. They must be 20,000 years old, for they spread over rocky clefts which have been broken up and hollowed out by erosion. Rex Gilroy, Director of the Mount York Natural History Museum at Mount Victoria, a respected archaeologist, discovered a giant footprint 1 foot 11 inches long and 7 inches wide in May 1970. The unknown youngster must have weighed 500 lb. The visitor can admire a plastercast of the dainty footprint, with corresponding stone hand-axes measuring 1 foot 3 inches by 7 inches, in the museum. On 2 April 1973, Rex Gilroy wrote to me: 'For example in the Blue Mountains of New South Wales I have discovered a series of primitive rock drawings and engravings of strange figures and unusual objects, which could only be described as spaceships, today, and had obviously been seen by the Australian aborigines.'

262

264

263

265

1

266

Moon City, the town of the Australian aborigines, lies north of Roper River in Arnhem Land. Moon City, also known as secret city, is like a copy of Sete Cidades. Similar 'streets' and smooth polished walls with peeled-off layers, the same impression of uncanny heat that must have raged here. Natural erosion, say the archaeologists, but there is no trace of erosion around Moon City. Legend has it that the sun god come here in his ship from heaven, that the earth god waged a barbaric war against him but was finally conquered by burning heat. One of the few visitors to Moon City, a reporter by the name of Colin McCarthy, claims that there is something strange about the place. Before him, a nun called Ruth was the only person to have penetrated the secret sector when she was invited by the seven oldest inhabitants of Moon City 30 years ago. She related that she was led into a cave, the walls of which were covered with drawings. When McCarthy arrived the caves and some remains of drawings were still there, but the interior seemed to have been destroyed by dynamite. The aborigines referred to an order from 'god' that after a certain time the writings had to be destroyed. They stuffed the cave full of the grass containing paraffin that grew nearby, set fire to it and pumped air into the blaze until the rock grew red hot. Then they threw water on it. The 'erosion' can now be visited.

262–265 Every Australian aboriginal tribe possessed a totem as a 'proprietary sign'. For example, a chieftain (262) wears a bird, symbol of flight, as a necklace, or hands cling to a bird body as if they wanted to hold fast to it while it flew (263), or a mask in the image of a God (264), and lastly a totem (265) with a floating being as tribal sign.

267

268

269

270

271

272

1

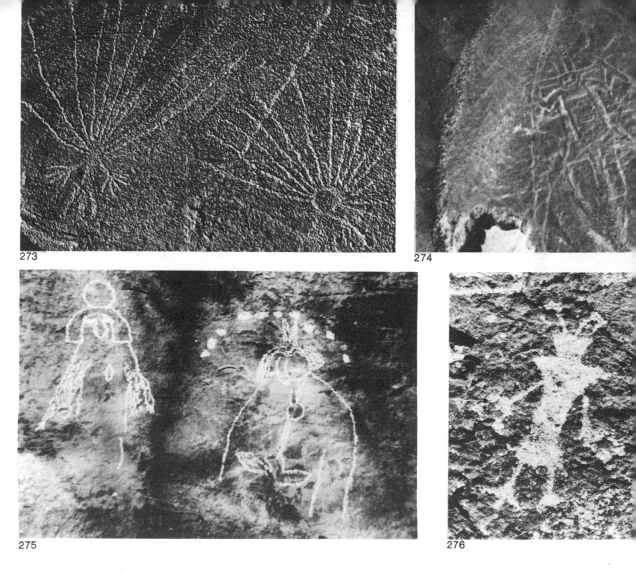

273

274

275

276

267–272 All these rock drawings come from Nevada, USA. They could all be examples of rock drawings all over the world. Were they the earliest communications to fellow tribesmen of contacts with extraterrestrial beings?

273 Here, 60 miles east of Alice Springs, near Ndahla Gorge, Australia, the aborigines engraved on the rock their leader's association with the cosmos.

274 The Indians did the same as the Australians on the rock faces around the plain of Nazca, south of Lima, Peru.

275 Similar images were made by Aborigines near the Blue Mountains in Australia.

276 And in the state of Utah, U.S.A. are to be found hundreds of petroglyphs of beings also wearing crowns of rays.

277

278

277–278 Both these rock drawings can be
seen in Arnhem Land, near Noorlangie,
Australia. The well-known periodical
National Geographic classified this find as
an aborigines' art gallery. Far, far away
from other Stone Age cultures, the round

heads with crowns of rays are repeated
here (277). A floating skeleton-like structure
with steering fins and antennae still awaits
cataloguing in one of the accepted
categories.

279

280

279–280 There is a distance of nearly 11,000 miles as the crow flies between the rock faces in Goiania, Brazil, and Laura, North Queensland, Australia. Nevertheless, the Stone Age painters chose the same motifs for their brushes: primitively stylised space-travel objects with steering fins. No bird can have served as a model for them. Did both Stone Age painters witness the same disturbing event?

281

281–285 A display of heads and suits, at least 8,000 years old. People have told me how I ought to interpret these drawings and how I must in no circumstances explain them. What I take for helmets and astronauts' suits are simply subjects taken from nature. Where did Stone Age painters from all corners of the world, quite indepently of each other, conjure up the same absurd manikin from? If these drawings are the result of sympathetic observation of nature, then the same manikin (with an astronaut's accessories) posed as model in North Queensland (281), in Nimingarra, Australia (283, 284, 285) and even in the Algerian Sahara (282). If anyone is interested in such fashion paintings I can supply the names of lots more open-air studios!

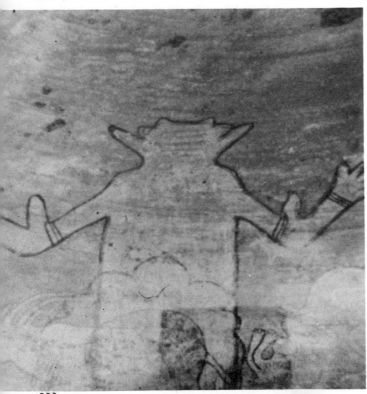

282

283

284

285

286

287

288

286–288 The Leyland brothers (286), who have been carrying out research in the Australian continent for years, find petroglyphs of the ancient inhabitants in astronauts' dress by the dozen. These two young scholars, well accustomed to the surprising by now, speak of zipp-fasteners as a matter of course when they describe this astronaut's gear (288). And Rex Gilroy, Director of the Mount York Natural History Museum, writes to me: 'I have made excavations during which a large rock plaque was unearthed on which were a number of strange human figures and something resembling a spaceship . . . I am in complete agreement with your theories about our prehistoric past.'

289

290

So far all attempts to capture signals from the cosmos with the aid of electromagnetic waves have failed. Dr George Lawrence of the Ecola Institute in San Bernadino, California, hit on a fantastic new way to communicate with extraterrestrial intelligences. Lawrence wondered if plants connected to an electronic control system would be suitable for communication with the universe. It is known that plants possess electrodynamic properties, indeed their capacity to assimilate tests and react in a binary way like a computer (go-no-go) is sensational. Lawrence closely observed the semiconductive and general electromotive capacities of plants. He asked himself the following questions as part of his programme:

1. Can plants be integrated with electronic apparatuses in such a way that they yield usable data?
2. Can plants be trained to react to specific objects or events?
3. Is the assumption that plants have the capacity for exceptional perception provable?
4. Which of the 350,000 kinds of plants is most suited for the test?

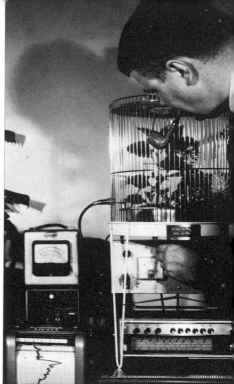

291

The smallest part of a plant is the cell. Cells react to heat and cold, radiation, damage, touch and light. Electric properties of cells can be **measured** with microelectrodes. If an electric current is passed through a plant, the cytoplasm contracts. Lawrence found that electricity had a polarising effect on spores and antheroids. If a plant (the mimosa pudica in the illustration) was damaged, it reacted with a measurable surge of current. This was called the nastic response, a reaction caused by fear which occurred especially in small plants. Large plants only reacted to large amounts of current. In the centre near Farmingdale where New York scientists examined plants for their potential use in space, genuine 'nervous breakdowns' were registered. Dr Clyde Backster, a lie-detector expert, observed similar effects in 1969. He attached a sensor to the leaf of a plant, while it was absorbing water. To speed up the reaction Backster was about to light a match. When he merely *thought* of this, the detector reacted immediately. The plant must have sensed his intention before it was carried out. As Backster thought it possible that the plant reacted telepathic-ally to men, he built an apparatus with which live shrimps were lifted out of cold water and plunged into hot water. A clock calibrated to a 100th-of-a-second registered on a graph the moment when the shrimps landed in the hot water. At the same fraction of a second all the plants in the vicinity reacted dramatically. This unexplained phenomenon was called the Backster effect. Dr Lawrence next tried to use plants for electromagnetic contact with the cosmos. A series of experiments, christened Project Cyclops, was organised over a distance of seven miles in the Mojave Desert, near Las Vegas. On 29 October 1971 at the same fraction of a second the measuring sets attached to the plants registered heightened curves which were transferred to a tape by an amplifier. What was going on? Was something underground stimulating the plants? Were there torrents of lava, earthquakes, magnetic influences? New sets were made, the plants were protected in lead boxes and Faradaic cages. The result was the same! Observed over a long period of time, curves and notes showed a certain synchronicity. The plants seemed to be communicating. Plants cannot think; they can only react. Every conceivable kind of magnetic wavelength was tried. At the moment of the different reactions, nothing could be heard. Could the process be connected with the fixed stars, with quasars or radiation? A new series of experiments clearly showed that the cause came from the cosmos. Radio-astronomers with their gigantic antennae could pick up nothing, but plants showed violent reactions. Obviously a wavelength that functioned *biologically* was involved. This brought the experimenters into a territory whose existence has been suspected, but which is not measurable so far – telepathy. A biological contact took place in a way unexplained to date, but during the detour via the cells it became measurable. Dr George Lawrence said on the subject:

Obviously biological interstellar communication is nothing new. We have only 215 astronomic observatories in the world, but about a million of the biological type, although we call them by other names such as churches, temples and mosques. A biological system (mankind) communicates (prays) to a far distant higher being. Biological understanding is also the order of the day in the animal kingdom; we have only to think of dogs and cats which find their way home again by instinct. A fascinating feature of the experiments in the desert is the realisation that these biological contacts with the cosmos are connected with the speed of light.

The suspicion is growing stronger that the plants are called up by someone in the constellation Epsilon Boötes at a hundred times the speed of light. That is also why radioastronomers could not register the transmissions. Why use a big drum when a kettledrum is available? Perhaps we have investigated interstellar contacts with the wrong instruments, the wrong wavelengths and the wrong spectrum until now. I asked Lawrence for his opinion about extraterrestrial visits and the amount of truth contained in myths. He answered:

The Chemehuevis Indians come from the Mojave Desert where I carried out my experiments. They belong to the linguistic family of the Mohaves, Cocopas, Halchidhomas, Yumas and Maricopas. A mythology which we tried to investigate relates that a 'humming star' came from heaven and landed in the desert. While the terror-stricken Indians watched the event, the 'humming star' burrowed into the ground and released streams of lava which originated the Pisgah and Amboy craters. We used geophysical magnetic measurements, but unfortunately we did not get any tangible results. At first we assumed that the spaceship, if it was one, had landed intact, with its engines running, so that today we could still register the magnetic field it left behind with a magnetometer. Secondly we started from the assumption that such a magnetic abnormality would also be measurable through rock and sand. A natural phenomenon spoilt the results. Molten lava, petrified in the sphere of the earth's natural geomagnetic field, produces a so-called 'thermo-remanent magnetisation'. Particles of lava react like trillions of individual polarised magnets. If the lava bed is very thick, the magnetometer only registers the lava, not the small magnetic field lying below it, with an intensity of 200 gamma or less. Nevertheless, I believe we are the first organisation to investigate scientifically with geophysical means whether there is anything tangible and still demonstrable in old legends. Our example shows that present-day methods are inadequate, especially when it is a matter of finding traces of intelligences more advanced than ourselves. This is not so much because scientists are unwilling to undertake such investigations, but because of the lack of equipment and the absence of technical and financial help.

292

In the autumn of 1972, John R. Tkach of Denver, Colorado, investigated the cities of Huayana Picchu and Macchu Picchu with modern measuring methods. Crystallography and infrared rays were used. The team, led by the geologist Dr White, came across a hollowed-out section of rock which reflected waves. John Tkach said of this phenomenon:

It consisted of a 6- by 6-foot semicircular parabolic reflector that was installed exactly above the upper ruins of the Second Tamus station. We arrived at the formula $Y^2 = 12X$. A mirror of this kind would not have been possible until after the analytical geometry of Descartes, around 1600. It is inconceivable that a primitive society could have built such a reflector without modern mathematics and modern tools.

1

For some strange reason the natives call it pampa, i.e. grassy plain, although there is not a trace of vegetation on the plain of Nazca, south of Lima, Peru. Lines run across the plain. Dead straight. For miles. They begin from nothing and end abruptly; some of them run parallel, others intersect. They climb straight up the next mountain peak and break off, yet seen from the air the plain looks as if it had once been a vast landing-ground. There are many explanations. The lines were Inca roads; they were connected with a religion of trigonometry, with an astronomical calendar, with a secret coded writing. I repeat that *it looks like* a landing-ground. What did they want wheels for? Their spaceships could function like a hovercraft. Why concrete? Because our landing-grounds are made of it? A layer of plastic, which would have disappeared after a few years, could have been laid equally well (and quicker). How plausible is the following idea? A supply ship left the orbiting command ship for our planet. It stopped on the plain of Nazca and left behind a track like skiers do in the snow. The strangers took off; another track was left. The natives hastened up. The 'gods' had been there and left traces behind! In the hope that the heavenly messengers would return they began to draw new lines and deepen the old ones. *That* is how the lines at Nazca originated, in my opinion. The gods did not show themselves. What had they done wrong? A high priest had a good idea. Priests always have good ideas. He said that they must show the heavenly ones sacrificial symbols. He urged his flock to scratch birds, fishes, monkeys and spiders among the system of lines – much enlarged so that they would be visible from a great height. That is *my theory* of the origin of the airport at Nazca! It is not necessarily right, but none of the previous explanations can claim to be the 'true' one.

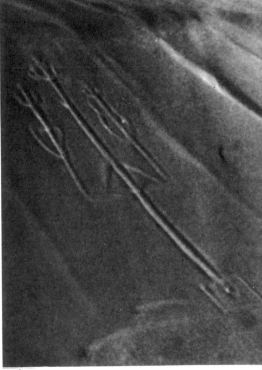

294

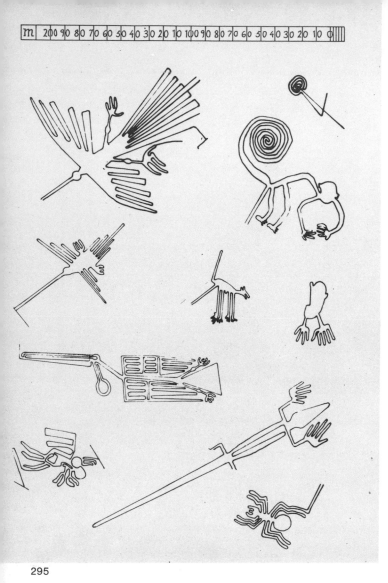

295

296

297

295–309 Side by side with the sketches (295) by the Nazca scholar Maria Reiche, the aerial photographs of the plain of Nazca tell such an obvious tale that any commentary by me is superfluous.

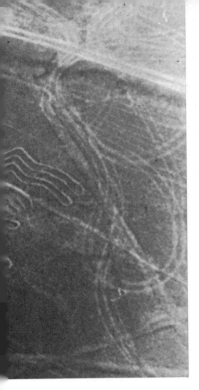

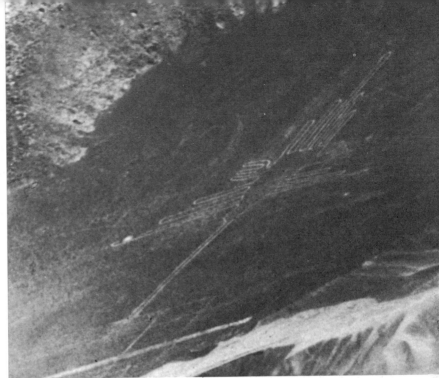

298

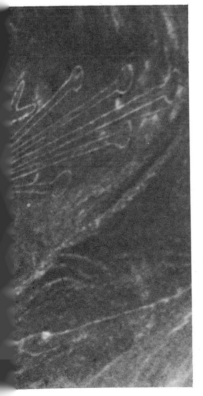

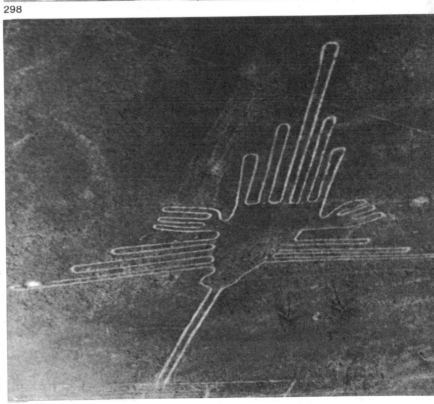

299

300

302

304

305

306

03
307

308

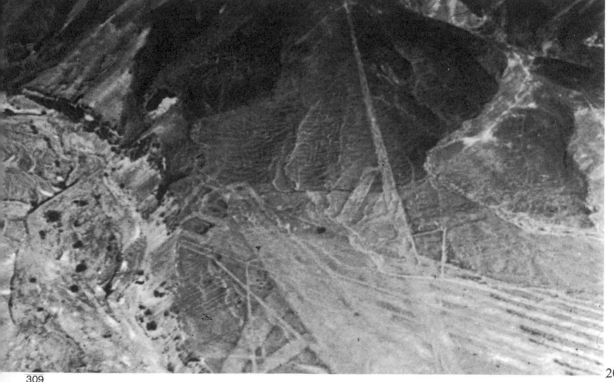

309

Today the greatest danger is people who do not want to accept that the age now beginning differs fundamentally from the past.

Max Planck

Location of the event: somewhere in the universe. Time of the event: thousands and thousands of our terrestrial years ago. Humanoid intelligences have reached a standard that makes interstellar space-travel possible. They possess tried and tested propulsion units, know the medical problems, know about time dilation on flights at high speeds and have satisfactorily solved all the problems of spacetravel. Where should they make for? The ideal goal would be a sun like their own, a planet that revolved within the ecosphere of its mother constellation and had similar gravitational conditions to the home planet. An ideal mixture of gases would be desirable, but not an absolute prerequisite. Do such planets exist? The strangers know that the statistical probabilities are high. If they also assume that all the matter in space was originally compressed into one lump, then all planets must have similar minerals and a similar life history. Although their temporal development may have been different, and different gases may have developed and finally dominated when they cooled off, a statistical 'degree of relationship' ought, at a conservative estimate, to show a million planets like earth in our galaxy alone. The search for a landing planet probably followed these lines: spectral analyses and the degree of magnitude of various fixed stars supplied values for related mother constellations; unmanned satellites radioed data about gravitational conditions from the solar system they had made their target. The locations of worth-while future homes were relayed back to the waiting emigrants. They did not want to travel just anywhere, they wanted a 'viable' planet. But why did the strangers want to travel between the stars at all? Why didn't they stay at home to solve the problems that doubtless existed there? Two questions, *why* does something happen? and *how* did it happen? have always been the stimulus for development and progress. Every intelligence owes its status to this stimulus. Questions such as *what happens where?* and *are we alone in the cosmos?* could have stimulated the extraterrestrial beings to make space travel their goal. Our present situation forces another thought, based on the results of research. At some point in time all the sources of raw materials will be exhausted, the planet will be worn out. Intelligent life with advanced technological knowledge would not acquiesce in such a realisation, it would mobilise all its abilities to find a chance of survival. It would not be afraid of using all the financial means and types of energy available. Seen like that, interstellar spacetravel (at that time in the future) would become a categorical imperative. Every sun in the universe dies one day, burns out in millions of years or becomes concentrated into a 'white giant' until finally it explodes as a *nova stella*. The more developed an intelligence is, the more carefully it would register all the changes in its mother sun. It would not want to die. It would try to prevent the knowledge amassed over thousands of generations from being wiped out at one stroke. This intelligence would strive to preserve its continuity. That supplies both purpose and goal of an interstellar journey. I assume the necessary technique for its execution as a premise. No one knows how many years the alien astronauts were under way, what time passed on their home planet, whence they came, at what speed the engine propelled the spaceship – yet many clever men have become convinced that on one day in our immensely remote past they entered our atmosphere, came in sight of the target planet. The spaceship swung into orbit round our world. Its crew mapped, photographed, observed and analysed it. This planet had a covering containing oxygen. Enormous forests alternated with oceans and deserts. The third planet was teeming with life. Hundreds of thousands of species of animals abounded on land and sea and one species was humanoid, like the strangers. These humanoids lived in caves, in groups. They had long shaggy hair and roamed from one feeding-ground to another. They possessed simple tools, but the race was dumb, stupid and grunted like animals. The only thing that frightened them was intruders.

The captain of the spaceship decided to give these people 'technical assistance'. He took the finest specimens and mutated their cells by artificial manipulation. The persons so treated were preserved for mating, but the willingly produced children were brought up on protected reserves. The offspring were incomparably more intelligent than their parents. Under the tutelage of the 'gods' they grew up in 'paradise'. In addition to language they learnt a useful craft. When the teenagers were pubescent, the captain gave them a warning lecture on these lines: 'You, my friends, are now the most intelligent creatures on this planet! You can rule over plants and animals. You can subdue the planet to your power. Only this commandment do I impose on you: never shall you mate with your former people who did not grow up in this paradise.' The reason for this warning was the captain's and the crew's knowledge that this new race could only become intelligent rapidly if they did not lapse into their primitive state, according to the laws of their previously dominant genes.

Speculation 1. When did all this happen? 30,000, 100,000 or 450,000 years ago? We do not know. Although we do not *yet* know what spacetravel technology was available to the extra-terrestrial visitors, where they came from and whither they were going, we do know for sure that until now the only explanations of the creation of mankind are religious ones. They cannot stand up to a convincing modern way of looking at things. It is a harsh fact that every theory of the origin of the species has a flaw *just where* it ought to explain convincingly how and why *homo sapiens* emerged from the family of hominids at such a rapid rate. Why did only one group of our ancestors become intelligent? Gorillas and chimpanzees, those amiable creatures so often ill-treated by animal collectors, belong to the self-same family as man, but I don't know any gorillas that wear trousers or chimpanzees that draw gods. On the other hand all the stories of the creation say that 'god' created man 'in his own image'. So, in spite of, or because of, all the attacks, I put the embarrassing question: when, why, through whom and for what purpose did man become intelligent so suddenly? So far I have not been lucky enough to get a sufficiently convincing explanation of man's becoming intelligent. The number of theories is like playing roulette. You pick your number but in the end you stand there empty-handed. Nothing is proved. Each find of a new skull provides the palaeontologists with new puzzles. Is it such an absurd idea that extraterrestrial beings intervened in the development of hominids by a planned artificial mutation at some early unknown date? Time dilation is a known fixed quantity for all present and future planned interstellar spacetravel projects. Couldn't the anthropologists, too, take notice of this scientifically verified fact at last? I know that this concept is hard to grasp and yet it is a fact. No eternity has passed for the 'gods' since their first visit to earth. They could be exactly the same crew that undertook the artificial mutation of hominids 100,000 or more terrestrial years ago and returned after thousands of years to inspire the results of their work. If that was so, the captain's horror is understandable. His creations had not kept the commandment he laid down. Instead of meeting an intelligent, technologically advanced race after thousands of years, the spaceship crew found hybrid beings of all kinds, contaminated, depraved, a terrifying mixture of intelligence and beast. What happened next?

Speculation 2. The captain decided to wipe out this wretched brood, with very few exceptions. What means were employed? It could have been done with fire, water or chemicals. The legends of mankind give many clues, such as the Flood or the destruction of cities from heaven (Sodom and Gomorrha), not to mention the overthrow of whole peoples by 'divine dust'. It is verifiable that at a given moment in time a tiny section of mankind suddenly produced writing, tools, technology, cultivation and mathematics. As long as I have to subscribe a fraction of belief to this phenomenon, I speculate that before he departed the captain left behind a groundcrew for other operations. They were entrusted with a number of scientific tasks, collecting data about the planets, studying the languages of different groups.

Then the worst happened! Perhaps the crew experimented of their own accord, perhaps the captain came back later than foreseen. At any rate the crew assumed that they had to spend the rest of their lives on earth. They mated with the daughters of earth. The prophet Enoch knew all about it. The captain made fun of him by saying that 'the guardians should watch over men, not vice-versa'. He says quite bluntly what he is talking about: '... slept with women, defiled yourselves with the daughters of men, taken wives unto yourselves and done like the children of earth and begat sons like giants . . . defiled yourselves with the blood of women, and begat children with the blood of the flesh, lusted after the blood of men and produced flesh and blood, as do they who are mortal and perishable.' My speculation goes further. The captain certainly did not unleash a deadly ray that would destroy mankind. Perhaps he dared not or could not take such a radical step, as children of his 'guardians' were already in existence. Legends also tell us that the heavenly ones took many men into their spaceship before they flew away. If they left a groundcrew behind, they obviously transmitted a tremendous amount of knowledge to mankind. Perhaps their feeling of superiority to the 'lords of the world' carried them away. Did they eventually fear the wrath of the captain and go underground?

The artificial tunnel system in South America might be a pointer in that direction. Or did the captain, as the myths relate, return after a losing 'battle in the universe' to seek safety among his own kind? If my version of mating between alien cosmonauts and the children of earth is accepted, the phenomenal puzzle of the dual nature of man is solved. As a product of this planet he is earthbound, as a coproduct of extraterrestrial beings, he is simultaneously 'son of the gods'. Man has never freed himself from this schizophrenic situation – half-beast, half-dreamer striving for the heavens. A part of this world-picture of mine is also the idea that our hominid forefathers experienced their time, the remotest past, directly, and absorbed it into their consciousness, storing up events in their memory. With each new generation a part of this primaeval memory was handed on, but every generation added its experience to the punched card of memory. Information was added to information. Perhaps in the course of time information may be lost to individuals or covered over by stronger impulses, but the sum of information does not decrease. In the perforations next to those of personal memories are the perforations of the 'gods' who were already travelling through space in Adam's day! Here we have reached the very point from which I claim that our whole future has already once been past. Whether we develop in a technical, biological or other conceivable way, what we shall find will already be the past, not human past, but the past of the 'gods'. It continues to affect us and becomes the present again every day. When a man has a brilliant idea today he has not discovered or invented it himself. He has dredged up basic information from the primordial memory to the surface of consciousness. The creative man of today must summon up knowledge from the punched holes of the remote past at the right moment. Past, present and future are united in an exhilarating way in the memory and mind of man. But since man became intelligent, since he could ask questions about his existence, origin and future, he has been programmed, in my opinion, to be 'space-ripe'. Suppose we dream that science has solved all the problems of this world, and revealed all the secrets. Then what? Would not people's eyes inevitably turn to the skies? It seems to me to be a human law to want to reach and investigate the cosmos. It is unimportant when this goal is finally reached. The stimulus is and remains the human wish for *peace*. Eugen Sänger said: 'The man who wants peace on earth, must also want space-travel'.

The first sentence of my first book said: 'It took courage to write this book.' And in spite of all the attacks I have not lost the courage, especially as I have been able to assemble more and more evidence to support my theories and speculations. As a child of my time, I consider looking at things with 'space eyes' more productive than appeals to faith. We should all like to know where we really come from, where we are going and what the meaning of life is. Will there ever by definitive proofs of my theories? I think and hope that there will. Victor Aubertin has expressed my hopes in an aphorism: 'Anyone who expects that something inside him will begin to think, will never think. One must want to think like one wants to pray and sing, to eat and drink.' We should simply be allowed to think, and speculation should be accepted as a fruitful part of thinking. If we were to reach a fixed star in a spaceship in a hundred years' time, practice artificial mutation on the inhabitants and return to earth, we should surely feel the need to leave signs of our presence behind. The plan would not easily be realisable. For one thing we should need a metal plaque that would last for thousands of years for the data we wanted to transmit. Once that was done, we should have to work out what data should be engraved on it and with what signs. We were here at this and that time. We found this and that. We came from a planet so many light years away. We left such and such a galactic system . . . We used propulsion units of such and such a kind . . . We set off again (or stayed behind) . . . We shall return in x thousand years at the earliest . . . Leave news for us at such and such a point. Such data would be necessary.

Where would we deposit them? We know as enlightened space-travellers that every planet has its wars, or natural catastrophies We could not safely entrust our 'testament' to a high priest or a chieftain. We know from our own history that the victors in battle destroy the sanctuaries of the defeated before anything else. Our plaques would be ruined. Should we bury them? Take them up to a mountain top? We would reject all these possibilities. The wrong people might find them at the wrong time. After long reflection, only one point remains, one logically mathematical point on the planet or in the heavenly machinery of the planetary system. Where could such a logically mathematical point on this planet be? The North or South Pole, for example. (So far no one has looked for traces of extraterrestrial beings at the poles!) A logical mathematical point in the celestial machinery? There is one point between earth and the moon where the gravitational fields of both heavenly bodies stop simultaneously. As earth and moon are constantly in reciprocal motion, that is the motions of the planets and the gravity of the sun have to be taken into account, the point would be a point on an orbit. But how by all the gods, should later generations get the idea of looking for proofs 'of a former visit from space' at such a point? As on a paperchase, clues must be scattered, indications that animate later generations to investigate a 'divine past'. Clues must find their way into holy books, be hidden in myths. They must astound the beholders in strange buildings that could not have been erected with the tools available to their ancestors. Lastly we would include all kinds of signs in drawings and reliefs to give a clue to the puzzle. Then we should die – in a hundred years perhaps. Visitors from outer space could have left signs of their early presence for us in the same way. Do such earthshaking proofs exist? Don't the sacred books constantly urge us never to tire in the search for truth? Doesn't the Bible say: 'Seek and ye shall find'?

Apart from a few experts, no one knows that an artificial satellite has been revolving in our solar system for 13,000 years. In December 1927 Professor Carl Störmer of Oslo learnt that the Americans Taylor and Young had received strangely delayed radio signals from space. Störmer, a specialist in electromagnetic waves, got in touch with the Dutchman Van der Pol at the Philips Research Institute in Eindhoven. On 25 September 1928 they undertook a series of experiments. Radio call-signs of different lengths would be radiated at thirty-second intervals. Barely three weeks later the same signs were re-registered on the receiver, but with delays of 3 to 15 seconds. The arrivals of the radio signals were registered with these intervals in seconds: 8 seconds – 11 – 15 – 8 – 13 – 3 – 8 – – 8 – 8 – 12 – 15 – 13 – 8 – 8. Thirteen days later, on 24 October, 48 more signs were received. Professor Störmer informed the scientific world of this in No 17 of *Naturwissennschaften* on 16 August, 1929. Then theories were propounded about how this delay in receiving short wave impulses could be explained.

Cosmic rays or reflections from the moon or other stars were thought of. None of the explanations was satisfactory. Why did echoes arrive at different intervals? The phenomenon was repeated in 1929 in 14, 15, 18, 19 and 28 February and then on 4, 9, 11 and 23 April. These echoes were registered all over the world by independent groups. Within a period of 16 minutes Professor Störmer noted these reception intervals: 15 seconds – 9 – 4 – 8 – 13 – 8 – 12 – 10 – 9 – 5 – 8 – 7 – 6 – 12 – 14 – 12 – 8 – 12 – 5 – 8 – 12 – 8 – 14 – 14 – 15 – 12 – 7 – 5 – 5 – 13 – 8 – 8 – 8 – 13 – 9 – 10 – 7 – 14 – 6 – 9 – 5 – 9.

In May 1929 the French radioelectricians J. B. Galle and G. Talon were on board the *Inconstant*. Their job was to investigate the effect of the curvature of the earth on radio waves. Their equipment consisted of a 500-watt short-wave transmitter with a 60-foot cable on a 24-foot mast. Various short signals were sent out, then the echo repeated itself. Between 15.40 and 16.00 their sign came back at intervals of from 1 to 32 seconds. There was no explanation this time, either. These observations were repeated in the years 1934, 1947, 1949 and in February 1970. Meanwhile the young Scottish astronomer Duncan Lunan had taken an interest in the phenomenon. As early as 1960 Professor R. N. Bracewell of the Radio Astronomic Institute of Stanford University, USA, had said that if an alien intelligence wanted to get in touch with us, it might possibly do so by the delayed return of radio signals. Duncan Lunan, President of the Association in Scotland for Technology and Research in Astronautics, made a serious study of the delayed signals. The result was staggering. Introduced into a second-grid, the signs received on 11 October 1928 produced an astronomical chart of the constellation Epsilon Boötes, 103 light years away from the earth. Lunan examined all the data from the 1920s and 1930s. A number of stars could be positively identified. From the measurements of the delayed echoes it was possible to assemble six astronomical charts, in each case enlargements of the constellation Epsilon Boötes. Asked about this phenomenon, Professor Bracewell said:

The maps produced on the basis of Lunan's analyses can be

adduced as a possibility of communication with another intelligence. When I want to tell someone whose language I do not speak where I come from, the best way to do it is with a picture. I am delighted that the British Interplanetary Society has examined this echo in such detail. The investigation could produce an overwhelming discovery. The satellite described by Lunan could never be seen even with the most powerful telescope. We cannot see our own spaceships in orbit round the moon with the most powerful telescope, either.

In *Spaceflight*, 1973, Lunan published the up-to-date results of his calculations under the title 'Space probe from Epsilon Boötes'. He came to the conclusion that an artificial satellite, which housed a complete programme of information for mankind, had been orbiting in our solar system for 12,600 years. The computer in the satellite was programmed so that it responded to radio waves from earth whenever its own position in relation to the earth was suitable for reception. The earth's signals were recorded and sent back on the same wavelength with intelligent delays. Sooner or later receivers on the earth would be bound to notice what was happening. Lunan thinks that to date we have received the following information from the unknown satellite in our solar system:

Our home sun is Epsilon Boötes. It is a double star. We live on the sixth of seven planets. Counted from the sun which is the larger of the two. Our sixth planet has one moon, our fourth planet has three and our first and third planets one each. Our satellite is in orbit round your moon.

It was possible to calculate the age of 12,600 years for the satellite by the constellation Epsilon Boötes. It is inconceivable for an interplanetary satellite to make a deliberate planned journey of 103 light years. If it flew under its own power, it would have needed incredible propulsion units. As the satellite is small, this possibility is excluded, quite apart from the fact that our astronomers would have seen a giant spaceship in lunar orbit. If the satellite started from Epsilon Boötes and flew to our planet in free fall, it would have been thousands of years under way, without propulsion and completely exposed to all the influences of gravity and the impact of meteorites. An alien intelligence that wants to (and can!) send information to another planet over a distance of 103 light years does not take a risk like that. The launchers of the satellite also knew that when it reached its goal, they would presumably no longer exist. Besides, at the launching untold millennia ago they could not have any idea that the earth, of all places, would harbour intelligent life in ages to come. One can accept a number of the facts as chances, but entry into orbit around our moon cannot have happened by chance. The satellite would have been attracted on entry into and passage through our solar system by larger heavenly bodies. This is my explanation. The artificial transmitting object was deliberately shot into lunar orbit by *someone* and this someone was here on earth 12,600 years ago. And then what? I think that the satellite has varied programmes for different branches of science: enlightenment for palaeontologists, astronomical charts for astronomers, help for geneticists and doctors, valuable knowledge for physicists. Lunan urges getting into laser contact with the satellite. If laser echoes, too, return to the transmission site at irregular intervals, the last dreamer would be forced to realise that terrestrial man is not the lord and crown of creation, and never was.

In *my world* alien astronauts lived on our planet thousands of years ago and our ancestors looked on them as 'gods'. They dictated the *whole truth* to earthly scribes and commanded them to hand on this *truth* unadulterated to future generations. The human failing of 'knowing better' distorted the truth. Religions came into being. Knowledge and truth were replaced by belief. The great majority of mankind still believes in a truth that is no truth. That is why I take the minor liberty of trying, with my theories and speculations, with the results of my researches and with my awkward questions, to bore through the blinkers which, forgive my saying so, most of us are still wearing.

310

311

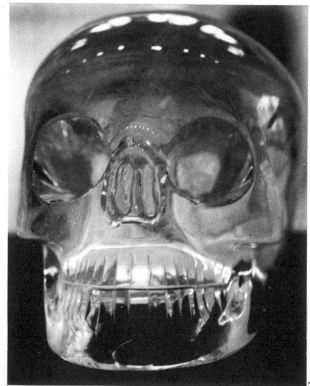

312

313

310–311 Two gold sculptures in the Museum of the State Bank, Bogota. One sculpture (310) gives the impression of a helmeted astronaut equipped with a pair of wings, while in my view the creature in 311 preserves the memory of an encounter with an extraterrestrial robot.

312 This head of pure rock-crystal was found in the Mayan ruins near Lubaantun (British Honduras). It weighs 11½ lb. Nowhere on the skull is there a clue showing that a tool known to us was used!

313 The face of an Indian is placed inside the corona of rays which surrounds the 'Sun God's' head. What is this combination of heavenly body and man meant to say? (Anthropological Museum, Mexico City.)

314

314–316   Three 'deities' wearing helmets (Anthropological Museum, Mexico City).

317

318

317 Once one disregards the figurative trimmings, we are left with a sketch of an electrical apparatus with electric circuits, etc. (Osiris pectoral, Tut-ankh-Amen, Thebes.)

318 The Goddess of Heaven, Nut, rises with bird's wings above the world she protects. References to flying are found in almost all Ancient Egyptian paintings and drawings. (Nut pectoral, Thebes.)

319

321

320

322

319–324 These are six of many, many illustrations from the
Dresden Codex (Sächsische Landesbibliothek, Dresden), but
they all look like technical drawings to me. I would merely

323

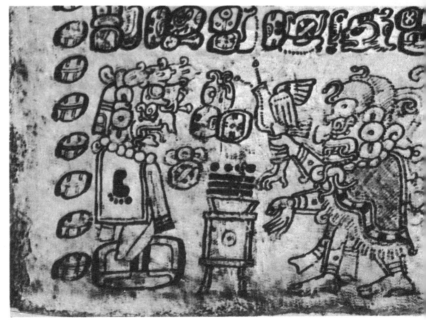

324

point out beings dressed like astronauts, motors worn on the back . . . and the fact that all the pictures have glyphs with numerals. The possible interpretations are endless.

327

325

328

326

325–330 These illustrations from the Madrid Codex are grist to my mill. They depict the whole arsenal of space-flight paraphernalia: supply systems, helmets with transmitters, an observer in a satel-

329

lite, and oxygen apparatus. And once again accurate numbers. So far only a minimum number of the Mayan picture writings has been deciphered, so there is plenty of scope for my assumptions.

330

331–335 These colour reproductions allow one to sense the material and imagine the subtle work of the Inca artists, and so receive something of the real impact of Father Crespi's work.

331

332

334

335

333

336

337

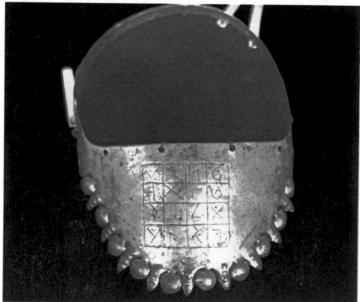

338

336 A stele with 56 signs still waiting to be deciphered. (337, an enlargement of the top two rows.) The signs fit evenly in the squares – so perfectly that they were probably as familiar to the artist as writing and came easily from his hands. The only snag is that so far scholars deny the existence of writing in pre-Inca and Inca times.

338 An Inca work that decorates the cover of this book – a necklace strangely ornamented with signs (writing?).

339–340 On my travels I kept on coming across extremely ancient spheres of all sizes. Do they preserve a memory of the 'Gods' who travelled in spheres? (Moeraki Beach, New Zealand; Maria Auxiliadora, Cuenca.)

339

340

341

342

341–342 Did extraterrestrial beings give our early ancestors sophisticated technical tools? When you walk through the caves in Ecuador and other South American countries, you can't help asking that question. The caves were certainly not the work of nature, which does not produce right-angled cuts, polished surface areas, extremely accurate grooves and straight corridors. These gigantic caves must have been cut out of the solid rock by tools that are quite unknown to us.

343–344 These interesting views of the underground cities at Derinkuyu, Turkey, show how they contrast with the caves. They were excavated with hammer and chisel by the sweat of men's brows. Astonishing subterranean structures, but nothing in comparison with the caves in South America.

343

344

345

346

347

345 Flying god in a sphere (Iraq Museum, Baghdad).

346 Flying Olmec deity at Teotihuacan, Mexico.

347 Flying snake, temple of Quetzalcoatl, Teotihuacan.

348 The Pyramid of the Sun at Teotihuacan covers an area of 50,000 sq. yards and is also laid out according to astronomical rules. We do not know in whose honour it was built.

349 The three ramparts of the Inca fortress at Sacsayhuaman are built of stone blocks, some of which are 18 feet high. The Sun God was worshipped there. 'Inca' means Son of the Sun.

348

349

350

351

352

353

350–351 There must have been an enormous layout here above Sacsayhuaman, which is already 17,800 feet above sea level. The phenomenon is explained as the effect of glaciation, but glaciers do not leave artificially worked stone behind or vitrifications that were produced at tremendous temperatures.

352–353 Statue of unknown god worshipped at Tiahuanaco and a parade of beautifully made monoliths. The incisions and indentations can be seen quite clearly, pointing to an architectural purpose. The age of the *technological* Tiahuanaco is unknown.

354

355

354–357 Nan Madol, a tiny island in the Carolines, houses an architectural complex made of 400,000 basalt blocks. No one knows how and why these stone blocks were brought from a neighbouring island to Nan Madol. One of the islanders' legends relates that a flying dragon helped with the massive transport job.

358

359

358–359 *Originally* the terrace at Baalbek was a technical structure. The Greeks and Romans built on a platform that already existed. The Russian Professor Agrest suspects that the original terrace was a landing ground for spaceships.

360–361 200 monsters like this guard the coast of Easter Island like menacing robots. It is not known whom they represent. The legends of the Rapanui, the original inhabitants, say that the statues marched to their positions using their own motive power.

362

363

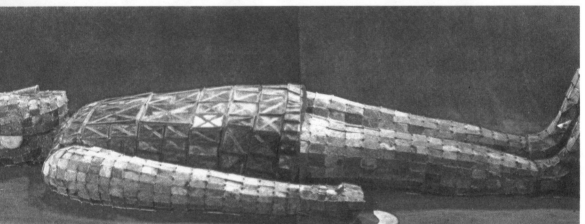

364

365

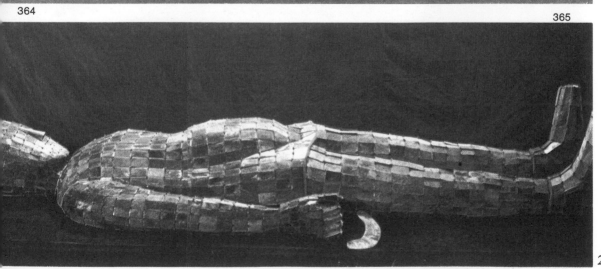

362–363 This Japanese Dogu sculpture, which is more than 5,000 years old, wears a helmet with big astronauts' goggles. Incidentally, goggles did not exist in the Japanese Stone Age!

364–365 'The mummies of a royal pair lay there in their funeral robes made of thousands of jade squares like astronauts in space suits,' wrote *Die Zeit* about these pre-Christian Chinese finds.

366–367 The American aviation engineer John Sanderson came to the firm conclusion that the gravestone at Palenque can be given a modern interpretation. And indeed the technical plan drawn by Sanderson clearly shows the purpose of all the outlines on the relief. Archaeologists should take the advice of engineers!

366

367

368

370

371

372

373

368–373 Aerial photographs of the landing grounds on the
plain of Nazca from the film CHARIOTS OF THE GODS.

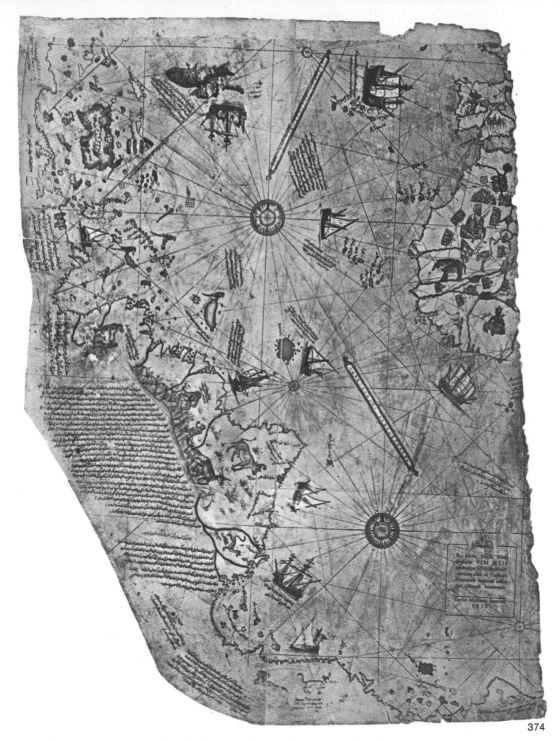

374   This is the original Piri Reis map of the world of 1513. At the lower edge of the picture it shows coastlines and islands of the Antarctic that were not discovered until our own day – 1952.

ARDREY, ROBERT, *African Genesis*, Collins, 1961.

BASS, GEORGE F., *Archaeology under Water*, Thames and Hudson, 1966.

BAUMANN, HANS, *Gold und Götter von Peru*, Güterslohe, undated.

BLAVATSKY, H. P., *The Secret Doctrine*, Vols. I-IV, Theosophical Publishing Co., London, 1888.

BUCK, PETER, *Vikings of the Sunrise*, University of Chicago Press, 1959.

CAMP, L. S. and C. C. de, Souvenir Press, 1966.

CATHIE, B. L., *Harmonic 695*, Wellington, 1971.

CHARROUX, ROBERT, *Le livre des secrets trahis*, Robert Laffont, Paris, 1965.

CHARROUX, ROBERT, *Histoire inconnu des hommes depuis cent mille ans*, Robert Laffont, Paris.

CHARROUX, ROBERT, *Lost Worlds*, Souvenir Press, 1973.

CHEN CHIH-PING, *Chinese History*, Taipeh, undated.

CHIANG FU-TSUNG, *The Origin and Development of the National Palace Museum*, Taipeh, undated.

CODEX TRO-CORTESIANUS, The American Museum, Madrid.

COMFORT, ALEX and others, *The Biological Future of Man*, Routledge, 1969.

CORDAN, WOLFGANG, *Das Buch des Rates, Mythos und Geschichte der Maya*, Düsseldorf, 1962.

COVARRUBIAS, M., *Indian Art of Mexico and Central America*, New York, 1957.

DÄNIKEN, ERICH VON, *Chariots of the Gods?*, Souvenir Press, 1969.

DÄNIKEN, ERICH VON, *Return to the Stars*, Souvenir Press, 1970.

DÄNIKEN, ERICH VON, *The Gold of the Gods*, Souvenir Press, 1973.

DARLINGTON, C. D., *The Evolution of Man and Society*, George Allen & Unwin, 1969.

DEUEL, LEO, *Flights into Yesterday*, Macdonald & Co., 1971.

DISSELHOFF, H. D., *Gott muss Peruaner sein*, Wiesbaden, 1956.

DISSELHOFF, H. D., *Das Imperium der Inka*, Berlin, 1972.

DITFURTH, HOIMAR VON, *Am Anfang war der Wasserstoff*, Hamburg, 1972.

EISELEY, LOREN, *Darwin's Century, Evolution and the Men Who Discovered It*, Victor Gollancz, 1959.

EISSFELDT, OTTO, *The Old Testament*, Basil Blackwell, 1965.

EMORY, K. P., *Stone Remains in the Society Islands*, Honolulu, 1933.

FERREIRA, MANUEL RODRIGUEZ, *O misterio do ouro dos martirios*, Sao Paulo, 1960.

GAMOW, GEORGE, *Biography of the Earth,* Macmillan & Co., 1959.

GAMOW, GEORGE, *A Planet called Earth,* Macmillan & Co., 1965.

GARCILASSO DE LA VEGA, *Primera parte de los comentarios reales, que traten del origen de los incas,* Madrid, 1722.

GRAND PALAIS, *Arts Mayas du Guatemala,* Paris, 1968.

HABER, HEINZ, *Our Blue Planet,* Angus & Robertson, 1971.

HAGEN, VICTOR VON, *World of the Maya,* New American Library, 1965.

HAPGOOD, CH. H., *Maps of the Ancient Sea Kings,* Turnstone Press, 1971.

HEYERDAHL, THOR, *Aku-Aku,* Allen & Unwin, 1958.

HONORÉ, PIERRE, *Das Buch der Altsteinzeit,* Düsseldorf, 1967.

HYNEK, J. ALLEN, *Unidentified Flying Object Experience,* Abelard-Schuman, 1972.

KIDD, KENNETH, *Indian Rock Paintings of the Great Lakes,* Toronto, 1962.

KRAMER, S. N., *History Begins at Sumer,* Thames and Hudson, 1958.

KRASSA, PETER, *Gott kam von den Sternen,* Vienna, 1969.

LEON-PORTILLA, MIGUEL, *The Broken Spears. The Aztec Account of the Conquest of Mexico,* Constable, 1962.

LUCAS, HEINZ, *Japanischen Kultmasken,* Kassel, 1965.

MARINS, FRANCISCO, *The Mystery of the Gold Mines,* U.L.P., 1961.

MONAD, JACQUES, *Le hasard et la necessité,* Paris, 1971.

NATIONAL PALACE MUSEUM, *Chinese Cultural Art Treasures,* Taipeh, 1971.

NEWMAN, ALFRED K., *Who Are the Maoris?,* Whitcombe & Tombs, Christchurch, N.Z., 1913.

PAHL, JOCHIM, *Sternmenschen sind unter uns,* Munich, 1971.

PARROT, ANDRÉ, *Sumer,* Thames and Hudson, 1960.

PARROT, ANDRÉ, *Assur,* Paris, 1960.

PAUWELS, L., and BERGIER, J., *Aufbruch ins dritte Jahrtausend,* Berne, 1962.

PAUWELS, L., and BERGIER, J., *Der Planet der unmöglichen Möglichkeiten,* Berne, 1968.

PAUWELS, L., and BERGIER, J., *The Eternal Man,* Souvenir Press, 1972.

PHILBECK, MAYNARD, *The Search for the Sun People,* Washington, D.C., 1968.

PHILIP, BROTHER, *Secret of the Andes,* Neville Spearman, London, 1961.

PRESCOTT, WILLIAM H., *History of the Conquest of Peru,* J. M. Dent & Sons Ltd., 1969.

RITTLINGER, HERBERT, *Der masslose Ozean,* Stuttgart, undated.

SAURAT, DENIS, *Atlantis and the Giants,* Faber & Faber, 1957.

SÄNGER-BREDT, IRENE, *Spuren der Vorzeit,* Düsseldorf, 1972.

SCHIRMBECK, HEINRICH, *Ihr werdet sein wie die Götter,* Düsseldorf, 1966.

SCHWENNHAGEN, LUDWIG, *Antiga historia do Brasil,* Rio de Janeiro, 1970.

SELIMCHANOV, I. R., *Ergebnisse von spektralanalytischen Untersuchungen an Metallgegenständen des 3. un 4. Jahrtausends aus Transkaukasien,* Baku, 1966.

SHKLOVSKY, J. S. and SAGAN, C., *Intelligent life in the Universe,* San Francisco, 1966.

STINGL, MILOSLAV, DR., *In versunkenen Mayastädten,* Leipzig, 1971.

SULLIVAN, WALTER, *We Are Not Alone,* McGraw Hill, 1966.

TEILHARD DE CHARDIN, PIERRE, *Man's Place in Nature,* Collins, 1966.

UMSCHAU VERLAG, *Die biologische Zukunft des Menschen,* Frankfurt am Main, 1971.

VALLÉE, JACQUES and JANINE, *Challenge to Science,* Neville Spearman, 1967.

VILLAS BOAS, O. and C., *Xingu,* Souvenir Press, 1974.

WATERS, FRANK, *Book of the Hopi,* New York, 1963.

WATSON, JAMES D., *The Double Helix,* Weidenfeld & Nicholson, London, 1968.

WEIDENREICH, F., *Apes, Giants and Man,* University of Chicago Press, 1946.

WIESNER, JOSEPH, *Histoire de l'art,* Paris, undated.

WIESNER, JOSEPH, *L'orient ancien,* Paris, undated.

WAISBARD, SIMONE, *Tiahuanaco,* Paris, 1971.

PHOTOGRAPHIC CREDITS

1 Werner Büdeler; 2, 9 Baghdad Museum; 3 Palestine Archaeological Museum; 4 National Museum, Teheran; 5 British Museum; 6 Metropolitan Museum, New York; 7 Thames and Hudson Ltd.; 8 Directorate of Antiquities in North Syria

10, 13, 15, 18, 19, 31 Louvre, Paris; 11, 21, 22, 25, 30, 32 Erich von Däniken (EvD); 12, 29 Oriental Institute, Chicago; 14, 20 British Museum; 17, 23 Berlin Museum; 24 Ankara Museum; 26, 27 Pierpont Morgan Collection; 28 Damascus Museum

33, 34, 40 Louvre, Paris; 34, 36 British Museum; 37, 38, 39, 41, 42, 44, 45 EvD; 43 Harvard Semitic Museum, Cambridge, Mass.; 46, 49, 50, 53 Constantin Film; 47, 48, 51, 52 J. F. Blumrich

54, 56 Constantin Film; 55 Ewing Galloway, New York; 57, 58, 59 Thames and Hudson Ltd.; 60 Louvre, Paris

61, 62, 63, 66, 67, 68, 69, 70, 71, 73, 79 Constantin Film; 64, 65, 74, 77, 78, 80, 81, 82, 88, 89 EvD; 76 London Express Pictures; 83, 84, 85, 86, 87 Pedra de Gavea, Photos Eduardo B. Chaves, EvD

90, 91, 92, 93, 100, 101, 104, 105, 106, 107, 107a, 109 Constantin Film; 95, 96, 97, 102, 103, 108, 110, 111 EvD

112, 113, 114, 115, 116, 117, 120, 121, 122, 123, 124, 125, 129, 130, 131, 132, 133, 134 EvD; 118, 119, 126, 127, 128, 135, 136, 137, 138, 140 Constantin Film; 141 Marcel Homer, EvD

142, 143, 144, 145, 146, 147, 148, 149, 150, 151, 152 Constantin Film; 153, 154, 155, 156, 157, 158, 159, 160, 161, 162 EvD

163, 164, 176, 177, 178, 179, 180, 181, 183, 184 EvD; 165, 166, 173, 174, 175 Constantin Film; 167, 169 Ernst von Khuon; 171 Catherine Krilrorian; 172 Charles Hapgood: *Maps of the Ancient Sea Kings,* Chilton Books, Philadelphia

185, 186, 187, 188, 189, 190, 191, 192, 193, 194, 195, 196, 197, 198, 199, 200, 201, 202, 203, 204, 205, 206, 207, 208, 209, 210, 211, 213, 214, 215, 216, 217, 218, 219, 220, 221, 222, 223, 224, 225, 226, 227 EvD

228, 229, 231, 232, 233, 238, 239, 240, 241, 242, 252, 253, 254, 256 EvD;
234, 235, 236, 237, 247, 248, 249, 250, 251, 255 Constantin Film

257, 258, 259, 260, 261, 262, 263, 264, 265, 266, 267, 268, 269, 270, 271, 272,
273, 275, 276, 279 EvD; 274, 282 Constantin Film; 277, 278, 280, 281, 286,
287 Leyland Brothers Films, EvD; 283, 284, 285, 288 Jon Noble, EvD;
289, 290, 291 Ecola Institute, San Bernardino, California, George
Lawrence, EvD

292, 293, 295 EvD; 294, 296, 297, 298, 299, 300, 301, 302, 303, 304, 305,
306, 307, 308, 309 Constantin Film

310, 311, 312, 325, 326, 327, 328 EvD; 313, 314, 315, 316 Constantin Film;
317, 318 Thames and Hudson Ltd.; 319, 320, 321, 322, 323, 324 Sächsische
Landesbibliothek, Dresden

329, 330, 331, 332, 333, 334, 335, 336, 337, 338, 339, 340, 341, 342, 350, 351,
353, 354, 355, 356, 357, 360 EvD; 343, 344 R. Rohr, EvD; 345, 346, 347,
348, 349, 352, 358, 359, 361, 362, 363 Constantin Film; 364, 365 New
Archaeological Findings in China, Peking

366, 368, 369, 370, 371, 372, 373, 374 Constantin Film; 367 John Sanderson,
EvD